M

KICKBOXING

DATE DUE

JAN 1 1 2007

KICKBOXING
The Complete Guide to Conditioning, Technique, and Competition

Christoph Delp

Foreword by **Martin Albers**

BLUE SNAKE BOOKS

Berkeley, California

Published by Blue Snake Books/Frog, Ltd.

Blue Snake Books/Frog, Ltd. books are distributed by
North Atlantic Books
P.O. Box 12327
Berkeley, California 94712

Cover photograph by Erwin Wenzel
Cover and book design by Brad Greene
Printed in Canada

Blue Snake Books' publications are available through most bookstores. For further information, call 800-337-2665 or visit our websites at www.northatlanticbooks.com or www.bluesnakebooks.com.

Substantial discounts on bulk quantities are available to corporations, professional associations, and other organizations. For details and discount information, contact our special sales department.

PLEASE NOTE: The author, the creators, and the publishers of this book disclaim any liabilities for loss in connection with following any of the practices, exercises, and advice contained herein. To reduce the chance of injury or any other harm, the reader should consult a professional before undertaking this or any other martial arts, movement, meditative arts, health, or exercise program. The instructions and advice printed in this book are not in any way intended as a substitute for medical care or mental or emotional counseling with a licensed physician or healthcare provider.

Library of Congress Cataloging-in-Publication Data

Delp, Christoph, 1974–
  [Kick-boxen basics. English]
  Kickboxing : the complete guide / by Christoph Delp.
      p. cm.
  Summary: "The complete guide to kickboxing, embracing all aspects of training, conditioning, and technique from start to competition with hundreds of photographs and detailed combinations of techniques"—Provided by publisher.
  Includes bibliographical references.
  ISBN-13: 978-1-58394-178-2 (trade paper)
  ISBN-10: 1-58394-178-9 (trade paper)
  1. Kickboxing. I. Title.
  GV1114.65.D45 2007
  796.815—dc22

                                                    2006031757
                                                         CIP

1 2 3 4 5 6 7 8 9 TRANS 12 11 10 09 08 07 06

Kickboxing

Kickboxing is a modern martial art, developed in the 1970s. In this sport, boxing and kicking skills are emphasized, and the level of success in competition is inspiring. Kickboxing is a popular method for fitness, competition, and self-defense.

Kickboxing develops the fitness components power, stamina, agility, coordination, and speed. Regular training improves your physical fitness, which can be maintained long-term.

As a competitive sport, kickboxing demonstrates numerous fascinating athletic capabilities. Athletes attack each other with fast boxing and spectacular kicking techniques. In addition, you can watch the Musical Forms version with athletes fighting imaginary opponents and giving perfect presentations of their technical skills.

Kickboxing techniques can also be adopted for self-defense. You can learn how to evade attacks and how to counter effectively. All athletes should pay particular attention to the training of all aspects of self-defense.

Table of Contents

Preface

Fascinated by the spectacular fights of top kickboxers, such as Don Wilson and Ferdinand Mack, I started kickboxing at a young age. Although I also spent some time in Thailand studying Muay Thai, I never lost my fascination for kickboxing.

I have only had the best of experiences with the Verband (Association) WAKO-Deutschland e.V. This applies equally to the Club Nippon Passau and to trainers Claudia Schregle and Markus Gattermann, with whom I trained as a young athlete, and also to the participation in the Budo Open. I am glad to have had the excellent cooperation of a number of outstanding WAKO athletes in the creation of this book.

Andreas Weingärtner, Jürgen Florian, Vanessa Florian, Martin Albers, Christoph Delp, Oliver Glatow, Natalia Hein, Giovanni Nurchi and Peter Zaar (from left to right).

Expression of Thanks

A heartfelt thanks to my family, and to all who have helped me in the preparation of this book: Martin Albers for the many bits and pieces of information and the composition of the team; Oliver Glatow and Eckhard Glatow for their assistance; Anastasia McGhee, Brad Greene, and Carissa Bluestone at Blue Snake Books; Peter Kruckenhauser (firm Budoland); Jens Walbersdorf (JEWA-media); Jürgen Schorn (WOK-Fotos) and Tom Schneider for providing photos; and, of course, the performers Natalia Hein, Vanessa Florian, Andreas Weingärtner, Christian Brell, Giovanni Nurchi, Jürgen Florian, Steffen Bernhardt, and Peter Zaar, as well as the young athletes Isabelle Eberling, Janine Steiner, Natascha Schuchardt, Filip Ajvasov, Nico Rings, Robin Neuser, and Peter Zaar, Jr. Working with all of you was a lot of fun.

—Christoph Delp, Bangkok 2006

Foreword

Dear Reader,

The sport of kickboxing is frequently shown in the media in a far too negative light. Time and again, you can see fights in back-alley arenas involving individuals with close links to the mafia and other gangs, participating in organized brawls.

This picture, however, very rarely bears any resemblance to the reality. Kickboxing is a sophisticated competitive sport, which is operated in accordance with latest findings in the area of sports science and organized by a democratically elected sports association, the WAKO-Deutschland e.V.

Kickboxing is an inspiring sport, and it quickly became the focus of my life. In the course of numerous contests in Europe, I not only got to know many interesting athletes, but also was able to compete with them under fair conditions. I do not find it hard to give back to the sport from which I received so much, and I am always eager to impart on upcoming young athletes what I gained from kickboxing: self-assurance, team spirit, and a comprehensive and balanced physical fitness.

Let the following pages convince you of the marvel of kickboxing. Christoph Delp's book contains a wide-ranging overview of the development of a young sport, and includes today's manifold and diversified types of training and competition.

Have fun reading and training.
—Martin Albers, Köln 2005

Part I
Background

Two competitors attack each other with lightning-fast boxing and kicking combinations, including thrilling roundhouse and jumping kicks. Impressed by the performance, the spectators wildly cheer on their favorite fighter.

This is the kickboxing we know from events, sports television broadcasts, and many action movies. In the following pages, you will learn how this sport originated and how it is practiced today. You will also get to know the basic techniques and training methods.

Book Structure

The first part deals with the different versions of kickboxing, the sport's history, and its most important rules and regulations. The second part explains how to find the appropriate training club or gym and reviews what equipment is used in kickboxing. In the third part, you'll learn basic skills, such as the fighting stance and footwork. The fourth part introduces the offensive techniques, and the fifth part explains how to develop these techniques and use them in different combinations. The sixth part discusses the basics of a strong defense and offers a selection of defensive and counterattacking techniques. The seventh part illustrates techniques for feinting, which will help you gain an advantage in a fight. The eighth part explains the training regimen for kickboxing, and includes training plans for beginners and advanced athletes. Finally, the ninth part is dedicated to the fight: conduct, tactics, weight divisions and preparation for a bout.

What Is Kickboxing?

Kickboxing is a modern, athletic form of the duel, wherein fists and feet are the weapons. Kickboxing was established as a competitive sport in 1974 with the objective that athletes in traditional martial arts, such as karate, tae kwon do, and kung fu, could compete in sports competitions using common rules and regulations.

Kickboxing is a strictly regulated sport, and much importance is placed on the respectful treatment of training partners, opponents, and fellow human beings in general. This training is not for hooligans—the sport's aim is the development of a calm, respectful demeanor, as well as superior physical fitness. As the body becomes fit, in fact,

aggression and anxieties should subside; however, should the occasion arise, kickboxing can be used as a strong self-defense method.

Kickboxing is a sport with mass appeal—it can be a hobby, a competitive sport, or a system of self-defense. All healthy people can practice this sport. Not everyone will know the glories of the ring, but a system of performance evaluation means that all practitioners can monitor their progress, and feel successful. Trainers periodically administer tests, and if the athlete passes the test, he or she is awarded a belt, which, depending on the performance standard, is colored yellow, orange, green, blue, brown, or black for the champion grade (DAN grades).

In order to appeal to all athletes, kickboxing is now being offered in **Semi-Contact**, **Light-Contact,** and **Full-Contact** versions. In addition, the World Association of Kickboxing Organizations (WAKO) stages tournaments in **Musical Forms** and **Aero-Kickboxing**.

Semi-Contact

In this version, opponents try to collect points by scoring successful hits. The techniques must be performed in a clean, controlled manner, and with light contact only. After each contact, the fight is interrupted and the technique used is assessed and scored. Contact with

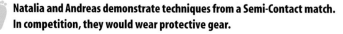
Natalia and Andreas demonstrate techniques from a Semi-Contact match. In competition, they would wear protective gear.

a legal target scores one to three points, depending on the technique's degree of complexity.

Light-Contact

In this version, opponents fight each other—making light contact—during a predetermined number of rounds. The fight is only interrupted after fouls, not after hits. Only clean and controlled techniques are granted points.

Light-Contact Kickboxing provides a good opportunity to prepare for Full-Contact Kickboxing, as it is a gentler form of the sport—control and precision, not knockouts or powerful techniques, are the aim. An athlete fighting with hard contact will receive a warning from the referee. Many athletes prefer this version to Full-Contact in the long-term.

Full-Contact

In this version, the fight is carried out with full contact over a predetermined period of time, in accordance with strict regulations on

 Tomasz Barada (right), an international kickboxing star, in a professional contest.

legal techniques and targets. The fight is decided by points or by knockout.

Originally, only punches and kicks above the hips were allowed in this version of the sport. But today you may see kickboxing matches that allow the low kick—a kick used in Thai kickboxing, a full-contact variant of Thailand's Muay Thai. Knee and elbow techniques, which you usually don't see in kickboxing matches, are also allowed in Thai kickboxing.

Aero-Kickboxing

As the name implies, Aero-Kickboxing combines kickboxing techniques with aerobics. This version is popular with fitness centers and aerobics studios, as its continuous rapid movements, carried out to the rhythm of music, burn high amounts of calories. Aero-Kickboxing is also offered as a competitive sport: aerobic teams present their programs (with background music) to judges.

A team performing an Aero-Kickboxing routine.

Musical Forms

This unique version features a sequence of forms, which the athlete uses to fight against one or more imaginary opponents. The fight is usually accompanied by music. There are four versions of the sport—two with weapons and two without.

Hard Style demonstrates predominantly "hard" techniques from karate and tae kwon do. **Soft Style** includes predominantly "soft" techniques from Wushu and Capoeira.

In **Hard Style Weapons**, practitioners use the following weapons: kama, sai, tonfa, yari, bo staff, three-part nunchaku, naginata, nunchacku, and katana. **Soft Style Weapons** utilizes the long stick, t'ai chi ch'uan sword, double sword, double hook sword, nine-part whip, and spear.

 Christian Brell (World and European Champion) and Steffen Bernhard (several-times German Champion) show techniques from their form program.

What can you gain from kickboxing?

Regular training develops physical fitness and helps maintain it long-term. It increases power, stamina, agility, coordination, and speed.

Kickboxing is well suited for weight-loss programs, because training sessions burn a high number of calories. If you combine this sport with healthy eating habits, you can easily reduce excessive body fat.

You can also fight everyday aggression and stress through intensive training (punching heavybags and focus mitts is especially therapeutic).

After a training session, you will often enjoy a renewed feeling of balance and satisfaction.

Regular training improves your self-confidence, too. Kickboxers know that they are able to handle self-defense situations and are not helpless victims. Positive feedback on your newly athletic form will also create satisfaction and self-confidence. Last but not least, you are bound to feel good in a healthy body that's full of energy.

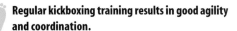 **Regular kickboxing training results in good agility and coordination.**

Who can train in kickboxing?

Any healthy person can try kickboxing. The training is suited for both men and women, and individuals of all ages can participate. Most kickboxing clubs offer courses for beginners, which progress slowly from basics to the more advanced techniques.

If you want to compete, however, you will be subject to the stricter rules and regulations in place to minimize the risk of injury to fighters. For example, to be able to participate in contact contests, athletes must prove that they have good vision and hearing. Age restrictions are in place, and contact contests have weight divisions. A medical examination prior to the fight is compulsory, as are regular check-ups between contests.

 **All age groups are represented in kickboxing.**

2

The History of Kickboxing

At the start of the 1970s, karate had become an international sport and was enjoying much media attention, thanks to its frequent appearance in Hollywood movies, namely those by martial arts legend Chuck Norris. However, karate contests left a lot to be desired—athletes competed without protective gear, and were therefore required to stop short before their moves made contact with a target. Injuries were common due to the difficulty of stopping fast and powerful techniques. Many athletes in all types of martial arts, including Bruce Lee, criticized this "artificial" fight style. Audiences, particularly in the United States, were little impressed by these fights, in part because they were used to the spectacular martial arts of the movies.

As a result of these objections, Jhoon Rhee, a celebrated martial arts master credited for popularizing tae kwon do in North America, developed protective equipment for the hands and feet, making contact contests possible. Meanwhile, an entrepreneur named Mike Anderson had already established himself successfully in the martial arts market. Together with his partners, one of them Georg F. Brückner, Anderson had the idea to market full-contact karate matches, which would utilize this new protective equipment. Tests showed that such contests were lively and spectacular, and carried minimal risk of injury to the athletes. Champions in all traditional martial arts could now compete and test the efficacy of their techniques.

In 1974, Anderson founded the Professional Karate Association (PKA) with his partners, and organized the first world championships in Full-Contact Karate (what kickboxing was referred to at that time).

These contests were met with great enthusiasm—13,000 spectators, including many celebrities, packed a Los Angeles arena. The preliminary fights in Berlin, organized by Brückner, had already been a great success, drawing 7,000 spectators. The first world champions in kickboxing were, among others, Bill Wallace and Joe Lewis.

In the years that followed, the PKA regularly organized major professional martial arts events in the U.S. Brückner, supported by many colleagues, staged many tournaments in Europe. Martial arts athletes from all traditional areas competed to test their skills.

Bill "Superfoot" Wallace became the first superstar of the PKA. He fascinated the audience with his spectacular kicks—which he performed despite a knee injury—and his intelligent fighting style. Another superstar of kickboxing was Benny "The Jet" Urquidez. He competed in many countries (Japan and the Netherlands among them), going up against local champions and fighting in accordance with the rules of their art. He was active for the professional World Kickboxing Association (WKA), of which his brother was a co-founder.

In 1977 the International Association World All-Style Karate Organization (WAKO), and its German branch, were founded in Berlin. (Some years later WAKO changed its name to World Association of Kickboxing Organizations.) Ever since WAKO's founding, many amateur and professional tournaments in semi- and full-contact versions have been staged on national and international levels.

WAKO's first amateur kickboxing world championships were organized in Berlin in 1978. One hundred and ten athletes from eighteen countries participated, and 8,000 spectators watched the event. Georg F. Brückner was once again the driving force behind the contest; he exerted a tremendous amount of energy and provided high financial investments to propel the popularization of this martial art. (Brückner passed away in his home town of Berlin in 1993.)

Although Full-Contact Karate had developed into a full-fledge international sport, WAKO had been at the time responsible only for amateur competitions. The professional side of the sport was eventually handled by the PKA and the WKA, though many other private individuals also founded professional associations against the backdrop of lucrative television contracts. The split was detrimental to kickboxing, as more and more title bouts of low quality were staged and shown on TV.

The second amateur World Championships took place in the U.S. in 1979. (At the time, the World and European Championships were both held annually; nowadays the World and European Championships alternate from year to year.) This time around, the previous superiority of the American athletes was no longer a factor, as most of their top athletes had turned professional. It was here that Ferdinand Mack won his first title in a full-contact sport; he is still WAKO's most successful amateur kickboxer to this day. He has also won many professional titles.

Don "The Dragon" Wilson won his first professional World Championship in 1979 at the age of 19, and in the next 20 years, he became one of kickboxing's greatest stars. He competed internationally, with varying rules, against the best athletes. One of his legendary fights was his win against Ferdinand Mack. He also acted in many martial arts movies, such as the "Bloodfist" films, and acquainted a large audience with kickboxing. He continues to appear in exhibition fights.

The 1980s saw regular Amateur World Championships in Semi-Contact and Full-Contact styles. In 1987 Musical Forms competitions were added to the WAKO championships. Light-Contact Kickboxing, which had been practiced in Germany since 1983, was included in the program of the World and European Championships in 1988.

The German WAKO-Pro was established in 1991, enabling the best WAKO athletes to compete for titles (and purses) in professional events without having to leave the association. The WAKO's international kickboxing program includes low kicks, and in 2000, WAKO also added Thai kickboxing and Aero-Kickboxing to the mix.

Development of Kickboxing Techniques

Kickboxing has adopted foot techniques from traditional martial arts, such as karate and tae kwon do, and boxing techniques from Western-style boxing. Traditional martial arts athletes, who competed during kickboxing's formative years, had to have realized that a change to their training was necessary if they wanted to pursue this new sport. Their former training structure did not enable them to fight with full power for several rounds. To build up the stamina needed for such a contest, athletes began to train intensively on equipment, such as punching bags, kicking pads, and focus mitts. Sparring was also added to the training regimen to further develop timing, stamina, and power—as well as to help athletes get accustomed to absorbing the force of their own hits and those they received from opponents.

Because the sport is so young, maintaining elaborate traditions is not a factor, as it can be in traditional martial arts. Against this backdrop, a sport based on modern scientific findings has emerged—a sport in which new findings can yet be integrated. Kickboxing is constantly evolving, and its athletes are constantly reaching new performance levels.

Kickboxing Today

Kickboxing has become an international sport. Millions of athletes practice kickboxing, and the number of members in the different associations continues to rise. This type of sport has huge potential on account of its positive effects on fitness, its spectacular competitive aspects, and its effective self-defense applications.

Large numbers of amateur athletes compete internationally in kickboxing tournaments. The professional contests, however, are usually attended by relatively few spectators; the purses, therefore, are usually small and only a few athletes manage to make a living as professional fighters.

The large number of professional kickboxing associations has had a detrimental effect on the spreading and popularity of kickboxing, as many professional bouts are staged with athletes who have not yet perfected their skills. Fortunately, these bouts rarely receive major media attention, as the participation of only the top athletes is a prerequisite for major televised events, such as Japan's "K-1."

In international terms, WAKO is still the leading kickboxing association. It has ninety member states on all continents, and more than one million active athletes in more than 6,000 clubs have joined the Association. WAKO is primarily interested in the sport and not in the financial gain of private individuals. In WAKO World and European Championships only one national team per country and only one athlete of the team per weight division may participate. In addition, the athletes must first qualify in national competitions.

WAKO is trying to make it possible for all its members to achieve their respective martial arts objectives by integrating many other arts, such as Thai kickboxing, into their programs. This move, however, comes with the risk of a further split in kickboxing that may have negative effects on its popularity and marketing. The inclusion of Muay Thai techniques, for example, cannot be viewed without some criticism. It raises the question of why athletes wishing to fight with elbows, knees, and other techniques specific to Muay Thai, should not simply switch to practicing that martial art. Kickboxing was originally meant to be fought solely with punching and kicking techniques (without low kicks)—and top athletes, such as Ferdinand Mack, thrill their audiences using only these techniques.

4

Important Rules and Regulations

In order to protect athletes from unnecessary injury, fights are subject to strict rules and regulations. The following is an overview of the sport's most important regulations, guided by the rules of WAKO Deutschland e.V. and WAKO World. Other associations may have slightly different regulations.

1 Medical Examination

Prior to the first contest, each athlete must pass a medical exam with a qualified medical doctor. The exam must be repeated on a yearly basis.

2 Clothing in Competition

In semi- and light-contact contests a quarter-arm t-shirt or jersey is used as a top. As an alternative, a kickboxing suit (similar to a karate uniform) may be worn. In Full-Contact bouts, men fight bare-chested, and women wear quarter-arm t-shirts or tank tops. For both men and women, kickboxing trousers must reach down to the ankles and must be held up by an elastic band around the waist.

In the Musical Forms version, athletes must wear clothing typical for the martial arts they incorporate into their performance: for example, in the Soft Style, athletes can wear Wushu suits or Capoeira pants with t-shirts. Clothing from different styles may not, however, be mixed together. In Hard Style, athletes perform barefoot; in Soft Style, martial arts sports shoes are legal.

3 Protective Equipment

In semi-, light-, and full-contact versions, athletes must wear a complete set of protective equipment. This includes a head guard, fight gloves, foot protection, shin guards, a mouth guard, and a groin protector. Women must also wear a chest protector. A list of legal protective equipment from a range of manufacturers can be obtained from the fight's promoter.

4 Weight Divisions

In contact kickboxing, the athlete's weight is checked just prior to the contest and the athletes compete in the corresponding weight division. The usual weight divisions for men, juniors, and women are as follows:

Semi-Contact and Light-Contact: Seniors and Juniors

Flyweight		up to 125 lb
Lightweight	above 125 lb	up to 139 lb
Welterweight	above 139 lb	up to 152 lb
Light Middleweight	above 152 lb	up to 163 lb
Middleweight	above 163 lb	up to 174 lb
Light Heavyweight	above 174 lb	up to 185 lb
Cruiserweight	above 185 lb	up to 196 lb
Heavyweight	above 196 lb	up to 207 lb
Super Heavyweight	above 207 lb	

Semi-Contact and Light-Contact: Women

Featherweight		up to 110 lb
Lightweight	above 110 lb	up to 121 lb
Middleweight	above 121 lb	up to 132 lb
Light Heavyweight	above 132 lb	up to 143 lb
Heavyweight	above 143 lb	up to 154 lb
Super Heavyweight	above 154 lb	

Full-Contact: Seniors and Juniors (Men)

Flyweight		up to 112 lb
Bantamweight	above 112 lb	up to 119 lb
Featherweight	above 119 lb	up to 125 lb
Lightweight	above 125 lb	up to 132 lb
Light Welterweight	above 132 lb	up to 140 lb
Welterweight	above 140 lb	up to 147 lb
Light Middleweight	above 147 lb	up to 156 lb
Middleweight	above 156 lb	up to165 lb
Light Heavyweight	above 165 lb	up to 178 lb
Cruiserweight	above 178 lb	up to 189 lb
Heavyweight	above 189 lb	up to 200 lb
Super Heavyweight	above 200 lb	

Full-Contact: Women		
Bantamweight		up to 105 lb
Featherweight	above 105 lb	up to 115 lb
Lightweight	above 115 lb	up to 123 lb
Middleweight	above 123 lb	up to 132 lb
Light Heavyweight	above 132 lb	up to 143 lb
Heavyweight	above 143 lb	up to 154 lb
Super Heavyweight	above 154 lb	

5 Fight Area

In Semi-Contact tournaments, the championship bouts are carried out on floor mats. Otherwise, they can also be carried out inside a marked area on the floor of a gym. The Light-Contact, championship fights take place in an area covered by floor mats or in a ring. Only regional tournaments can also be carried out on the floor of a gym. Full-Contact championships are staged in a ring. Tournaments for juniors can also be carried out on floor mats. Musical Forms require an area of at least 10 m x 10 m.

6 Fight Time

Semi-Contact and Light-Contact fights are usually scheduled for three rounds of two minutes each. The clock is, however, stopped in the event of injuries or hits. In both versions, the fight time in tournaments can be reduced to two rounds of two minutes each. Full-Contact amateur fights are always scheduled for three rounds of two minutes each. There is a break of one minute between rounds.

A Musical Forms performance may last for a maximum of two minutes and fifteen seconds.

7 Legal Techniques

Throughout the entire length of the fight the athlete must land both hand and foot techniques to receive points. Jabs, hooks, and upper-cuts are permitted fist techniques. The backfist may also be used in Light-Contact matches. The ridgehand strike may be added in Semi-Contact. The spinning backfist is not allowed in some versions and by some associations.

The front kick, back kick, roundhouse kick, hook kick, crescent kick, ax kick, and footsweep can be used as foot techniques. Foot techniques can also be carried out after rotation and as jumping kicks. In addition, low kicks can be used in Full-Contact. Thai kick-boxing permits elbow and knee techniques. Three acrobatic exercises are allowed in the Musical Forms as additional techniques.

8 Legal Attack Targets

In most bouts, the head can only be attacked from above, the front, or to the side, though in Semi-Contact matches, the back of the head may also be attacked. The upper body can be attacked from the front and the side. The feet may only be attacked by the footsweep technique from the inside or outside up to the height of the ankles. In Full-Contact matches with low kicks, and in Thai Kickboxing, the legs may also be attacked (at mid-thigh range).

9 Forbidden Attack Targets and Fouls

You are not allowed to attack the back of the head (except in Semi-Contact). Athletes may not use techniques on the neck, throat, genitals, back, legs (except in Full-Contact with low kicks and in Thai kickboxing), and joints.

The athlete is not permitted to attack if the opponent gets stuck with one leg between the ropes or if any one part of his body, other than his feet, touches the floor.

The athlete may not turn his back to the opponent, run away, fall down intentionally, kneel on the ground, or the like, in order to interrupt the fight.

The athlete may not use any throws or wrestling techniques. The spinning backfist is also forbidden in some matches.

No further techniques are allowed after the bell has rung to signal the end of the round or after a referee commands you and your opponent to stop the fight.

Talking in the ring, and unsportsmanlike conduct, such as biting and spitting, will be disciplined accordingly. Contraventions, depending on the type of violation, will be penalized by a warning, point reduction, or disqualification.

10 Scoring

In Semi-Contact matches, all clean techniques that make light contact with a legal target are awarded one to three points according to the degree of difficulty.

In Light-Contact and Full-Contact contests, ringside judges score each round individually. They evaluate hits, the quality and difficulty of the techniques employed, the fighters' overall strategy and demeanor, and minus points (for fouls or other violations) to reach a final score for each round. A premature end of the fight by knockout is only possible in Full-Contact bouts.

In the Musical Forms version, the "fight" is also judged on the variety and difficulty of the techniques used. Elements of the traditional fighting techniques, such as power and tension, are included in the judgment. In the weapon versions, the athlete must demonstrate perfect execution of the techniques and total control over the weapons used.

11 Medical Care and Precautionary Suspension

Contests can only take place when a medical team is in attendance. In Full-Contact, the presence of a doctor is obligatory. If the medical team or the doctor has to leave the event temporarily, the contests must be interrupted.

The medical team must examine any athlete who has taken the full count after a big hit, and must then decide on subsequent medical measures. After a knockout or a technical knockout stemming from too many hits to the head, an athlete will automatically be subject to a suspension. The athlete's fitness must then be re-examined by a doctor before he or she is allowed to compete again.

Part II
Getting Started

Training
Objectives

5

You can train in kickboxing for many reasons: to improve your fitness, to compete on an amateur or professional level, or to practice self-defense. Steady training will help you to become a good kickboxer. However, whether or not you can also be a successful competitive athlete depends on your physical preconditions.

Kickboxing as Fitness Training

Kickboxing provides an excellent opportunity to improve physical fitness, lose weight, and reduce stress. If kickboxing is your main form of exercise, you should train at least twice a week to improve your cardiovascular fitness. If you are already physically active in a different sport, it suffices to train once a week. If, however, reducing body fat is your primary aim, you should be active in the sport at least five times a week, including two to three kickboxing sessions and two other sessions of either stamina or power training. In addition, you should adhere to a balanced, healthy diet—if you don't eat well, you can't expect to lose weight no matter how hard you train.

Many fitness centers offer different types of aerobic kickboxing courses, which will allow you to improve your fitness. It should be noted, however, that when it comes to precision of form and/or self-defense applications, these classes are not suitable substitutes for training at a real kickboxing gym.

If you are interested in learning the intricacies of the sport while you get in shape, visit several kickboxing clubs and choose the one at which you feel most comfortable. Concentrate initially on the basics of kick-boxing, before you settle on a version (semi-, light-, or full-contact).

Kickboxing as a Competitive Sport

No matter which style they choose—Semi-Contact, Light-Contact, Full-Contact, Thai kickboxing, Musical Forms—athletes start out by competing in regional contests. These contests allow them to qualify for national championships. Only the best athletes can participate in World Championships.

If you want to compete in regional amateur contests you must train at least two to three times per week. For a fight in contact kickboxing you must also train for stamina and power, watch your diet, and, if so required, lose weight in order to compete in the most suitable weight division. For participation in national and international championships, however, this level of training intensity is no longer sufficient, due to the large number of talented athletes.

Professional athletes must concentrate fully on kickboxing. They must be technically perfect, as the opponent will exploit every weakness and return with hard counterattacks. In addition, they must be in optimum physical shape, have no deficits in power and stamina, and maintain a low proportion of body fat. All of this requires a minimum of five specifically tailored training sessions per week, plus several additional power and stamina sessions.

To achieve success as a competitive athlete it is essential to find a knowledgeable trainer and good training partners.

Kickboxing as Self-defense

Kickboxing trains the use of—and the defense against—hard punches and kicks. Athletes learn to perform these powerful techniques from a distance; they also get used to absorbing hits, so that they may avoid the state of shock that can accompany an attack. Not all techniques that are generally taught as self-defense apply to kickboxers: for example, ground-fighting techniques are not included, and elbow and knee techniques are only trained in Thai kickboxing. These should not be seen as omissions—rest assured that kickboxing offers a dynamic system of self-defense. Bear in mind that in an emergency, parts of the body that are considered illegal targets in the ring (such as the groin area) may be attacked.

Kickboxing trainers must be aware of the difference between sport and self-defense. It is, therefore, recommended that kickboxing training should be enhanced by self-defense lessons. Self-defense techniques should be practiced at the end of a training session or in separate sessions. The trainer is then better able to go into all aspects of self-defense, which include how to avoid emergency situations and how to defend against an attack from any distance. Understanding the self-defense aspects of the sport makes a kickboxer a complete martial artist.

Kicks to the groin are not allowed in sports competitions. However, in a life-threatening situation they are an appropriate means of defense.

One of the great things about kickboxing is that it's not necessary to master a large number of techniques to handle an emergency situation. You must learn to keep an attacker at a distance, which can be done with straight punches and kicks, and you must learn to incapacitate the aggressor from a short distance, which can be done by employing knee and elbow kicks, or holding him or her tight using lever techniques. Once these techniques are learned by heart, they can be carried out instinctively.

Lever techniques and elbow techniques can be used for self-defense.

Interview with Martin Albers,
World, European, and German Champion

Where did your interest in kickboxing come from, and at what age did you begin training?

My brother Michael and my father Helmut introduced me to kickboxing at the age of 14. Michael had already been training with Jochen Böckmann in Cloppenburg, Germany. It was a baptism by fire: in one of my first training sessions, my brother gave me a black eye. This, however, could not stop me from further kickboxing training. Along with kickboxing, I regularly participated in tae kwon do training with Jochen Böckmann.

Have you always been agile? How long did it take until you were able to execute high-kicking techniques and kicking techniques after rotation?

As a child I spent much time on the soccer field. Due to my rapid growth during puberty, and also on account of my soccer training, I developed major deficits in coordination and agility. Jochen Böckmann always emphasized intensive stretching and kicking training, so that I progressed quickly. The combination of hand and foot techniques was a great advantage in that particular phase of my growth, so that I was able to improve my coordination deliberately in and outside the area of sport. After two to three years, it was no particular effort to perform jumping kicks to the head, even after rotation.

When did you have your first fight and how did it end?

I competed in my first tournament in 1991 in Dalfsen, Holland. As a yellow belt, I narrowly defeated a blue belt in All-Style Karate. My next contest was not as successful. For the next feeling of success, I had to wait more than 18 months. However, my patience, in combination with the motivation I received from my trainer Jochen Böckmann, finally paid off.

What about your subsequent career? How much success did you have?

Until 1997 I competed predominantly in Semi-Contact and/or All-Style Karate contests. My success rate was average. Then, Peter Zaar trained me to become a contestant in Light-Contact, in which I quickly proved to be successful. After some initial podium positions in WAKO tournaments in 1997, I had my breakthrough in 1998. This was followed by success in the German Championships and, to my surprise, also in the European Championships in Leverkusen. In the next few years, I won more titles in the German and European championships. I became World Champion in 1999.

How did you prepare yourself for contests?

My trainer Peter Zaar organized his training sessions in accordance with the WAKO-Deutschland e.V. schedule of contests and tournaments. The season starts in January with comprehensive basic training, conditioning, and coordination exercises—jogging tests and power sessions make up the core activities of this phase of training. This is followed by special basic training in February. Finally, the kickboxing equipment comes back in use to practice conditioning exercises on a punching bag or with a training partner. This phase is supplemented by initial rounds of sparring, which are subject to certain restrictions in order to develop certain skills.

The actual preparation for contests starts in March. Apart from speed units, you concentrate on many rounds of sparring. In addition, the training is supplemented by particular tactical and strategic elements.

I continued to add to the regular training by participating in group jogging sessions and doing additional "homework" given to me by my trainer. In the peak tournament season I was, therefore, busy with one or two daily kickboxing or conditioning training sessions.

Did you ever suffer any severe injuries in training or competition?

Throughout my active competitive career I was very lucky to not suffer from any serious injuries. Superficial injuries, such as a black eye or sprained toes, were rarely able to stop my training.

The best prerequisite for training safely is to invest in high-quality equipment, which all athletes should own. The trainer of the German National Team, Peter Zaar, always claims that the best possible protection is just good enough. Very few injuries are reported from his training sessions.

What are your plans for the future? Do you want to stay active in kickboxing?

I concluded my career as an amateur kickboxer in 2002 after winning my third title as European Champion. Currently, I have no offers for an attractive title bout in the professional arena; however, on this level I could imagine some events in the coming years.

What is your advice to beginners with competitive aspirations?

Most important is patience and regular training. "From yellow belt to World Championship" has already been Georg F. Brückner's motto. This I can only emphasize, because comprehensive technical training of the basics combined with good stamina and the right frame of mind form the foundation of a successful competitor.

A beginner should not harbor any false ambitions and rush into fights too early. An athlete training in regular intervals cannot avoid becoming a good kickboxer one day. With a little luck and reasonable ambitions, competitive success may be possible at some stage.

The beginner should also receive adequate advice from his or her trainer on competitive rules and regulations. The referee's directions must be clearly understood and followed. In addition, prior to a contest the athlete should determine with his trainer the aim of the fight. Even though the referees of the WAKO-Deutschland e.V. are of a very good standard, the time at which the towel should be thrown in ought to be discussed, particularly before the initial contests.

6

Rules of Conduct

Kickboxing teaches its practitioners to treat fellow human beings with respect. Kickboxing offers a person a physical advantage over untrained individuals, but its techniques may never be used to bully others; they are to be applied only in self-defense or for the protection of others. Anyone who learns kickboxing with the aim of serving his or her egoistical interests should be expelled from training.

Conduct in Training

Students must be punctual. If a student is unable to arrive on time to a training session, he must notify the head of his group and excuse himself for being late.

An athlete's appearance must be neat, and he or she should wear clean clothes for training. Items such as rings, necklaces, and watches must be taken off prior to training.

Loud laughter and exclamations should not occur during training. Generally, discussions should only be held in reference to the training.

Students must follow the trainer's instructions at all times. Questions may, of course, be raised during training, and the trainer should resolve genuine communication problems, but students should be mindful to not monopolize the trainer's attention. The trainer has only a certain amount of time for the session and must also take care of other students; further questions can be followed up on after class.

Students must treat each other with politeness and respect. Hurting your training partner is never acceptable. The aim of a session is not for one student to demonstrate superiority over another, but for all students to cooperate, so that all can achieve a higher performance level. If your partner does not adhere to this principle, goes too hard when sparring, or tries to consciously inflict injuries, you should first try to discuss it with him or her. If his or her behavior doesn't change, find a new training partner. If your trainer insists that you continue to "brawl" with this partner, you have chosen the wrong club.

Conduct During a Fight

Opponents welcome each other before a fight to show respect for each other as athletes. However, once the contest begins, the aim is to win, which means athletes may now start to do whatever serves this purpose, provided it conforms to the rules. This may involve intimidation tactics in contact kickboxing, such as aggressive stares. Certain provocations are not acceptable, though. These include insults, spitting, and the conscious use of forbidden techniques (e.g. attacks to the groin). If a fighter persists with such antics, he will be disqualified.

After the fight, the athletes say goodbye to each other in a warm and respectful manner. Both have given their best, and both must respect that.

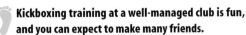
Kickboxing training at a well-managed club is fun, and you can expect to make many friends.

Martin presents the equipment he uses for competition. Normally, he wears his groin guard and shin guards under his pants.

7

The Athlete's Equipment

The following equipment is used for kickboxing training. For your first training session, you can wear long training pants and a t-shirt. Most clubs have a basic assortment of public-use equipment. If you decide to train for an extended time period, however, it is worthwhile to acquire your own equipment. Your trainer can help you choose the products best suited to your training goals. Frequently, trainers have deals with equipment producers and can help you obtain products at favorable prices.

Clothing

Kickboxers generally wear short cotton t-shirts or train bare-chested. Special long pants, made of nylon, cotton, or satin, are also part of the uniform. These pants are available in specialty martial arts shops. Kickboxers often train barefoot, as shoes can be a hindrance when learning kicking techniques, and wearing shoes during partner drills or sparring increases the risk of injury to your training partner. In competition, clothing varies depending on the version of kickboxing.

Hand Wraps

Wrapping the hands helps to prevent injuries to the knuckles and other joints—it is highly recommended in training, and required in competition. For training purposes, you may use either longer, bandage-like white wraps or shorter, standard wraps similar to the ones that boxers use. These shorter wraps come in different colors, and sometimes have built-in loops that fit over the thumbs.

In competition, long, white, bandage-like wraps of a specific style and length are required. The trainer wraps the fighter's hands and a fight official closely examines the finished job to ensure that the fighter enjoys the best possible protection.

Gloves for Heavybag Training

Bag gloves, which are smaller and lighter than the boxing gloves used in sparring or fighting, are required for training on heavybags, speedbags, pads, and focus mitts. You can also use boxing gloves, which are heavier and bulkier, but bag gloves are the standard for equipment training, and are far less expensive than boxing gloves. Also, when training with a partner or when in competition you may only use gloves that are practically new (using damaged gloves raises the risk of inflicting injuries on your partner or opponent), so you're better off buying bag gloves, which can withstand daily wear and tear, and saving your boxing gloves for sparring only.

Boxing Gloves

Sparring with training partners requires 16- or 18-ounce boxing gloves. Smaller and lighter boxing gloves (8 oz or 10 oz, depending on which weight division the fighters are in) are worn in contests. Boxing gloves used in competitions are subject to stricter regulations than gloves used in daily training; therefore, the production of gloves for competitive fights is more expensive, which, in turn, is reflected in the price.

Mouth Guard

You must wear a mouthpiece during contact training or competition. Mouth guards protect you from losing teeth, fracturing your jaw, and, depending on the style of the guard, may protect you from concussions brought on when the lower jaw slams into the upper jaw. For optimum protection, a mouth guard must be molded exactly to the shape of your teeth. Most brands are made of plastic that softens enough in hot water for you to mold them to your liking. The least expensive shields only fit around the upper teeth—for the best protection, spend a little more money on a guard that also protects the lower jaw and provides a better cushion between the two. You can even obtain a mouth guard from your dentist, molded from a dental impression, but these are very pricey.

Groin Protector

A blow to the groin, whether intentional or unintentional, can result in serious injuries. This is why a groin protector must be worn in competition and during contact training. The simplest models are reasonably priced, but the more expensive models, particularly those for professional kickboxers, can be pricey.

Head Gear

You should wear head gear during sparring—or during any training where hard blows or kicks to the head are practiced. Head gear, though required for amateur fights, is not used in professional contests. Intensive boxing sparring warrants the purchase of a very thick, high-quality head guard.

Foot and Shin Guards

In training you can opt to use foot and shin guards. These guards are compulsory for amateur contact fights. They are sometimes allowed in professional fights, but only by certain organizations.

Peter Zaar, German national trainer in Light-Contact Kickboxing, displays his training equipment: targets and a kicking shield.

8

The Trainer's Equipment

A kickboxing trainer uses different types of pads to teach both individual techniques and combinations. If he's working with an advanced athlete, the trainer will also use the pads to generate situations that resemble a real fight. He can simulate, for example, an opponent's attack by approaching the athlete with raised pads. The athlete must then step out of the way or deliver a number of techniques into the pads to stop the trainer from advancing farther. The trainer also has the opportunity to withdraw, thereby inviting the athlete to follow with the use of techniques. Newcomers shouldn't attempt these fight simulations—if either training partner is inexperienced, the danger of injury is too great.

The following pieces of equipment are usually available for public use at most clubs; however, these pieces (especially Thai pads) often see heavy use, and advanced athletes often like to purchase their own to ensure that they're training with the best possible equipment. Some Full-Contact trainers also use thick foot and shin guards for the intensive training of kicks and low kick blocks.

Focus Mitts

Focus mitts are small pads held in the hands. They are particularly suited for teaching punching techniques, and they are important tools for boxers. They are not suited for training powerful kicking techniques, as the pads are too thin to safely absorb that great of an impact. Moreover, there is always the danger that the technique may miss the pads or slip off, thereby hurting the trainer.

Targets: Combined Punching and Kicking Pads

These pads are suitable for all punching and kicking techniques. The pads are made of Bayflex®, a highly elastic polyurethane foam. Top Ten®, a German company, makes these training aids, which are available in the U.S. through specialty dealers.

Thai Pads

Thai pads are long and thick pads, specifically developed for professional Muay Thai training in Thailand; they enable the high-power use of all the body's weapons.

Though plastic pads with air fillings are available, leather pads with solid fillings are recommended for both men and women. The use of an air-filled pad is not recommended for intensive training, as the kicking athlete will not get a chance to toughen up his shins and feet, and the trainer must endure the full impact of the hit.

Kicking Shield

A kicking shield is a large pad, which is held in front of your body with both arms. It is particularly suited for side kicks and back kicks. For example, a large number of such kicks can be carried out with power and in succession, thereby building up the respective groups of muscles.

Part III
Basic Knowledge

How to Begin

Beginners must first learn the correct **fighting stance (starting position)**. From this stable position, you can ward off the opponent's techniques and stage counterattacks.

Once a student has perfected the fighting stance, he or she must practice **footwork** (moving around while maintaining the fighting stance). A student practices moving to the front, to the back, and to the side—this will constantly change the **fighting distance,** thereby robbing the opponent of a fixed target. As long as the athlete is within the fight distance, he must always maintain his fight position.

Only after mastering the initial stance and footwork . . . will a student start to learn offensive techniques. Each technique is first practiced by itself, before it is incorporated into combinations. Once the athlete has learned a large number of offensive techniques, he or she begins to practice a selection of defensive and countering techniques. The student's repertoire will be expanded slowly, step by step, to ensure the development of a good athlete.

Fighting Stance

Kickboxing typically has two different fighting stances: the front stance and the side stance.

In Full-Contact and Light-Contact matches, the fight lasts over a number of rounds. The referee only interrupts the contest if the rules have been broken. A large number of combinations are carried out, and an athlete is best able to perform these while in the **front stance**. In this position, the athlete usually keeps his stronger arm (this will most likely be your right if you are right-handed or your left if you are left-handed) behind the weaker arm, close to his or her face. The weaker arm is generally used to set-up various techniques, often by initiating a short, quick jab to distract the opponent.

In Semi-Contact, the fight is interrupted after each hit. Therefore, the **side stance** is particularly suited for this variation, as this position makes it possible to land swift hits. The athlete frequently fights with the stronger part of his body pointing toward the front.

Front stance (left) and side stance (right).

Front Stance

In the front stance the athlete usually keeps the stronger hand behind the weaker one, and close to his or her face. This way you can start combinations with the weaker hand and then follow-up using the powerful techniques of the stronger hand. This strategy is particularly important in Full-Contact.

Right-handed students take the conventional stance, putting the left hand (the weaker one) forward. Left-handed students fight in the "southpaw" stance (i.e., they hold the right hand in front).

The following describes the conventional stance. This applies in reverse to southpaws.

Stance

Right-handers step the left foot forward, left-handers the right foot. The front foot points toward the opponent or is slightly turned in. The rear foot is turned about forty-five degrees to the side, pointing away from the front foot. The front foot rests fully on the floor, with most of the weight on the ball of the foot. The heel of the rear foot is slightly raised. The weight of the body is evenly balanced on both feet.

Guard

Keep your body erect. Tuck your chin toward your chest. Hold your front hand at eyebrow level, and hold the rear hand slightly above your jawline. Your muscles, especially those in the shoulder, should be relaxed. In the beginning, it is difficult to maintain this hand position over an extended period of time—keeping your arms raised in this manner quickly tires out the muscles. But after a few weeks of regular training, the muscles will be stronger.

Giovanni shows the front stance.

Look

Direct your gaze toward your opponent's chest and torso, but do not focus on one point: try to see the entire body. This way, you are best able to anticipate his or her next move. At close distance, you should direct your look toward the opponent's head.

Side Stance

This stance facilitates side kicks and backfists, and is best suited to Semi-Contact contests, which are interrupted after each point. Athletes frequently turn the stronger side of their bodies toward the front, so that they can use their best techniques early in the fight. However, this means that an athlete must work hard to try to mislead his or her opponent, hence, why many athletes change their stance several times throughout the round. Some athletes, however, prefer to use a karate stance in Semi-Contact.

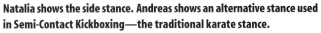 Natalia shows the side stance. Andreas shows an alternative stance used in Semi-Contact Kickboxing—the traditional karate stance.

Stance

The feet are parallel and the lower body is sideways, angled toward the opponent. The weight of the body is evenly distributed to both feet, and the knees are slightly bent.

Guard

Turn your upper body toward the opponent. The front arm guards the part of the body pointing toward the opponent, and the rear hand is next to the head. Keep your muscles relaxed, particularly the shoulder muscles.

Look

Again, direct your gaze toward the center of the opponent's body, but do not concentrate on one point: try to look at the entire body. At close distance, direct your gaze toward the opponent's head.

11

Footwork

Once you have mastered the fighting stance, you can start learning footwork. These steps are used to approach an opponent, to turn back, or to step out of the way in order to avoid him.

Whenever you move around the fight area, you should always remain in the fighting position. Stay relaxed and don't neglect your guard. Move on the balls of your feet for quicker action. When you stop moving, your feet should be back in the starting position.

Initially, beginners should practice footwork as a separate unit, done in addition to the regular training sessions. Perfecting these movements is the prerequisite for the effective use of both offensive and defensive techniques. If, for example, you want to bridge the distance to the opponent in order to use an offensive technique, you must take a quick step forward, all the while remaining in your fight stance.

To train footwork, it's best to determine a fight area (i.e., the size of a ring) to use for practice. When you come close to the edges of this field, you should move away using side steps.

Forward Step

From the fighting position, move the front foot forward, resting the ball of the foot on the floor. Do not take a big step—the movement should be between a step and a sliding motion. Now follow with the rear foot, so that you resume your fighting position.

Rear Step

From the fighting position, move the rear foot back, resting the ball of the foot on the floor. Now follow with the front foot, so that you resume the fighting position.

Side Step to the Left

From the fighting position, move the left foot to the left, resting the ball of the foot on the floor. Now follow with the right foot, so that you resume your fighting position.

Side Step to the Right

From the fighting position, move the right foot to the right, resting the ball of the foot back on the floor. Now follow with the left foot, so that you resume your fighting position.

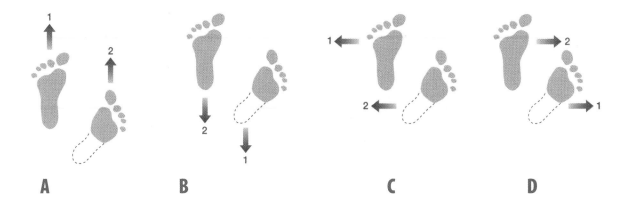

A   B   C   D

12

Fighting Distance

The fighting distance refers to any distance that puts you within reach of your opponent. No direct techniques can be delivered at a distance of more than approximately five feet between individuals of average height. The attacker must first take a step in the direction of his opponent, or he must jump toward him, before he can use a technique. The opponent, however, can avoid the fight by taking one step back or moving to the side.

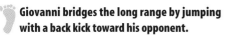

Giovanni bridges the long range by jumping with a back kick toward his opponent.

If fighters are close enough together to use techniques, they are in the so-called fighting distance. The fighting distance is divided into three groups: long range, half range, and close range.

Long Range

Kicking is the predominant method of attack at long range—namely front kicks, side kicks, and jump kicks. To use a punching technique, you must first take a step forward. A suitable way to bridge a long distance, or to move away from the opponent, is to combine the step with a jab (using the forward hand). By using a hard kicking technique, you can move the opponent out of the immediate fighting distance.

Half Range

Both punches and kicks can be used at half range. Aggressive kickboxers look for the opportunity to attack their opponents with many different combinations. To avoid such an attack, you can try to move back and out of this distance, or you can narrow the distance with a step to the front in order to clinch. Advanced kickboxers frequently watch each other at half range and try to determine the strength, weaknesses, and reactions of their opponents.

Close Range

Close range is mainly used for hooks and uppercuts, and knees and elbows (if you practice Thai kickboxing). These techniques are carried out continuously, and until such a time that one of the fighters succeeds in moving away or getting hold of the opponent.

Hook kick at half range.

A hook at close range.

Legal Targets

In kickboxing events governed by the WAKO, fighters are permitted to use legal fight techniques to the following parts of the body:

- The head may be hit from above, from the front, or from the side.
- The upper body may be attacked from the front and the side.
- The feet may only be attacked for sweeping from the inside and outside, up to the level of the ankles.
- In Semi-Contact, the rear of the head may be attacked.
- In Full-Contact with low kicks, and in Thai kickboxing, the thighs and lower legs may be attacked.

Particularly Effective Points of Attack

1. Temples

2. Area around the eyes and cheekbones

3. Nose

4. Lateral center of the lower jaw

5. Tip of the chin

6. Area around the collarbone

7. The upper arm (right below the shoulder)

8. Solar plexus

9. Lower ribs

10. Stomach

11. Outer thigh muscles (particularly at the mid-thigh mark)

12. Feet

Bear in mind that within different kickboxing associations and types of kickboxing some differences exist in respect to the legal impact points. Remember that a knockout is only the aim in full-contact sports.

1 Temples

A blow to the temples will daze an opponent and can also cause a knockout. Recommended techniques are the hook, the roundhouse kick, the hook kick, and the crescent kick.

2 Area around the Eyes and the Cheekbones

Hard blows here result in swelling. This area must be hit hard and hit frequently, so that the swelling can force the fight to end. Techniques that can be used are the jab, the rear straight punch, and the side kick (with the heel).

Stabbing the eyes—for example, with the thumbs—is strictly forbidden in competitive sports.

3 Nose

A hard blow to the nose causes pain, dizziness, and bleeding. However, the opponent's pain and bleeding, even in the event of a broken nose, is often not strong enough to stop the fight. The straight punch and the side kick are the best techniques to injure the nose. You can also hit the nose with an ax kick.

4 Lateral Center of the Lower Jaw

The lower jaw contains numerous nerve endings. Hard impact here can easily lead to a knockout. Techniques are particularly effective if the opponent's mouth is open, and the jaw, thus, not fixed. For this reason, you must always keep your mouth closed when sparring or fighting. Recommended techniques are the hook and the hook kick.

5 Tip of the Chin

The chin has nerve endings that may cause unconsciousness when hit. The best technique is an uppercut delivered to the underside

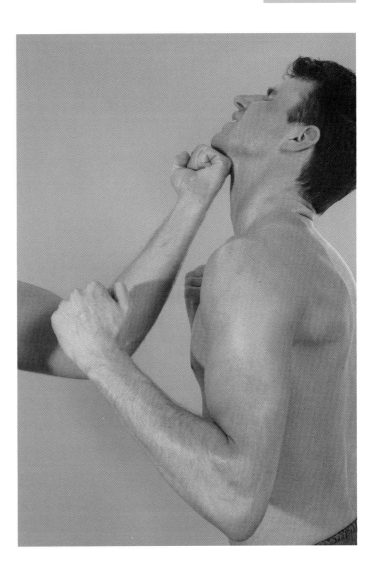

An uppercut to the chin.

of the chin. For this reason, you must always remember to keep your chin tucked toward your chest when sparring or fighting. In addition to the uppercut, you can also use the straight punch, the front kick, and the side kick to attack the chin.

6 Area Around the Collarbone

Hard blows to this area cause intense pain. If the collarbone is fractured—which, mind you, is not the objective of a fair kickboxing contest—the opponent will experience pain strong enough to make the use of the arm on this side of the body impossible. The area can be attacked by techniques from above, for which the ax kick is a suitable weapon.

7 The Upper Arm

A hard blow to the upper arm (just below the shoulder) or to the inner side of the upper arm can lead to short-term paralysis symptoms—your opponent will be unable to move his or her arm for a few seconds. Techniques that use hard and small contact areas are the most effective, for example, a kick that uses the heel as a striking surface. Punching techniques can also be effective, but they are not easy to execute during fights due to the comparatively large and soft contact areas of boxing gloves.

8 Solar Plexus

A hard technique to the solar plexus will make the opponent feel dazed and causes dizziness. You should use a technique that delivers maximum impact, for example, a straight punch from the rear, a front kick, or a side kick.

9 Lower Ribs

The area around the lower ribs is a good target to use during contests. Hits cause pain and breathlessness. After several hits, the opponent is fighting for breath and is unable to continue. It is, however, rare that the first hit results in a premature end of the fight. For this reason, you must continue with other techniques. You can deliver the hook, the uppercut, and the roundhouse kick to the lower ribs.

10 Stomach

A blow to the stomach can cause great pain and nausea, and can knock the wind out of your opponent. This is why it's important to strengthen your stomach muscles so that you can tense them and absorb the impact. To the stomach, you can deliver the straight punch, the uppercut, the front kick, the side kick, and the back kick.

The bladder is located between the stomach and the genital area. Even though it is not a permitted attacking target, it may be hit during a contest, and possibly overlooked by the referee. Blows to the bladder cause strong pain—the bladder could even burst. The risk is particularly high for a full bladder, which is why you must always empty your bladder prior to a contest.

11 Outer Thigh Muscles

This target is only legal in kickboxing matches that use low kicks and in Thai kickboxing. Hard kicks result in strong pain. Such a technique can lead to paralysis symptoms and floor the opponent, who may be unable to continue the fight. For maximum impact, kicks should be delivered to the mid-thigh. Note that it is never legal to deliver low kicks to the knee.

 A roundhouse kick to the ribs.

12 Feet

For a footsweep, the feet can be attacked from the inside and outside, up to the level of the ankles. The attack causes the opponent to lose his balance, and he can then be targeted efficiently with further techniques. A footsweep can also result in a hard fall to the ground, which may potentially injure the opponent.

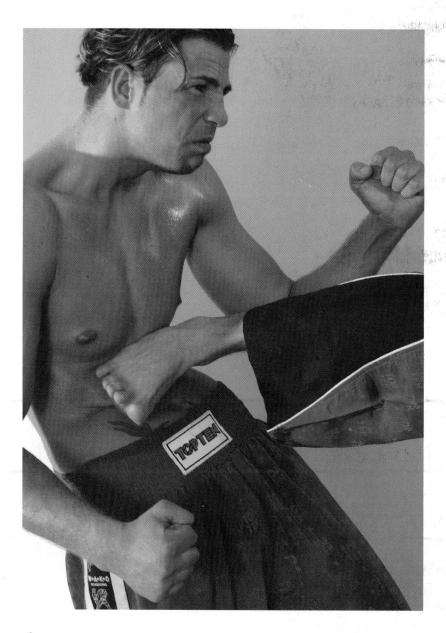

A side kick to the stomach.

Part IV
Offensive Techniques

14

Introduction

Once you have mastered the **fighting position** and **footwork,** you can start to learn **offensive techniques**. It will, though, take some time until you have adopted all the techniques. For example, high-kicking techniques require an agility that may take some time to acquire, whereas rotation or jumping techniques require intensive training to build up the requisite coordination and power. The answer to the question of how long it will take for you to master these techniques depends on how regularly you train and on your overall level of health and conditioning at the time you begin training.

You need not master all techniques in order to participate in kick-boxing contests. The techniques used in competition must, however, be powerful, quick, and precise, as the opponent may otherwise be able to counter effectively. The more of the following techniques you can employ, the more difficult it will be for your opponent to figure you out.

Dominik Haselbeck lands a hook to the body during the 2005 World Championship in Nuremburg, Germany.

15

Punching Techniques

This chapter will introduce you to the techniques most frequently used in kickboxing contests. Bear in mind that regulations differ from contest to contest. The spinning backfist, for example, is not permitted by all associations.

Punch

1.	Front Straight Punch (Jab)
2.	Rear Straight Punch

Hook

3.	Front Side Hook
4.	Rear Side Hook

Uppercut

5.	Front Uppercut
6.	Rear Uppercut
7.	Uppercut to the body

Backfist

8.	Backfist
9.	Spinning Backfist

A

B

C

1. Front Straight Punch (Jab)

Targets: Nose, Chin, Eyes

Execution:

Start off in your fighting stance. Raise the heel of the front foot slightly, and send the front fist toward your opponent in a straight line. You should keep your elbow tucked down as long as possible; otherwise, you will "telegraph" the punch, meaning your opponent will notice your technique at an early stage and will be able to defend himself. The rear fist remains in the starting position—slightly above the jaw in order to protect you from your opponent's techniques. As you throw the jab, turn your hip slightly and shift your weight to the front leg for maximum power. Shortly before you make contact, turn your fist so that your palm is facing the floor. After throwing the punch, quickly return the fist to the starting position.

A–C: *The straight punch with the front arm is also referred to as a jab. Use the punch as often as possible, to distract your opponent and disrupt his or her timing.*

2. Rear Straight Punch

Targets: Nose, Chin, Eyes, Solar Plexus, Stomach

Execution:

Again, start off in the fighting stance. Raise the heel of your rear foot slightly, and propel your rear fist toward your opponent in a straight line. As with the jab, you should keep the elbow tucked in as long as possible; it's very easy to telegraph a right straight punch. Keep your front fist above your jawline for protection against your opponent's techniques. As you throw the punch, turn the hips, and pivot on the rear foot—this will shift your weight to the front for a powerful execution of the technique. Shortly before making contact, turn your fist so that your palm is facing the floor. Make sure that this punch is explosive—don't just push the arm out, but really use the power generated by the motion of your hips. After throwing the punch, quickly return the fist to the starting position.

A–C: *Giovanni demonstrates the rear straight punch.*

A

B

C

A

B

C

3. Front Side Hook

Targets: Jaw, Temples, Ribs

Execution:

Starting from the fighting position, swing your front fist sideways—so that the arm is nearly parallel to the ground—as you shift your weight to your front leg and lean your upper body slightly to the side. Keep your other fist above the jawline in order to block possible techniques from your opponent.

Carry out this lateral punch by turning the body and rear hip in the direction of the punch, while shifting your weight in the same direction. After throwing the punch, quickly return the fist to the starting position and get back into your fighting stance.

A–C: *The side hook with the front arm.*

4. Rear Side Hook

Targets: Jaw, Temples, Ribs

Execution:

Starting from the fighting position, raise your rear fist sideways, so that the arm is nearly parallel to the ground. At the same time, shift your weight to the rear leg and lean your upper body slightly to the side. Keep your other fist above the jawline to protect you from your opponent's techniques. Follow through with this lateral punch by turning the body and the hips in the direction of the punch and shifting your weight in the same direction. After throwing the punch, quickly return the fist to the starting position.

A–C: *The side hook done with the rear arm.*

A

B

C

A

B

C

5. Front Uppercut

Targets: Chin, Ribs, Solar Plexus

Execution:

Start off in the fighting position. Drop your front arm and turn your fist so that the lower and the upper arm form a rough right angle. For this technique to be effective, you must shift your weight to the front leg and bend your knees somewhat. The other fist is kept above the jawline for protection.

Now, explode into the technique from below: pivot your body and hips and shift your weight to the front as you straighten the legs. Make sure that you hit the target square with the knuckles—and that the punch is not interrupted on the way up. Quickly return the fist to the starting position, and retract back into your fighting stance.

A–C: *Vanessa demonstrates the front uppercut.*

6. Rear Uppercut

Targets: Chin, Ribs, Solar Plexus

Execution:

Start in the fighting position. Drop your rear arm and turn your fist so that the lower and the upper arm form a rough right angle. As you do this, shift your weight to the rear leg and bend your knees somewhat. Keep your other fist above the jawline for protection.

Now, explode into the punch from below, as you pivot your body and hips, shift your weight to the front, and straighten the legs. Make sure that you hit the target with the knuckles—and that the punch is not interrupted on the way up. Quickly return the fist to the starting position, and get back into fighting stance.

A–C: *The uppercut with the rear arm.*

A

B

C

A

B

C

7. Uppercut to the Body

Targets: Ribs, Solar Plexus, Stomach

Execution:

Starting off in the fighting position, drop one of your arms (the technique works the same way on either side) and turn the fist so that the lower and the upper arm are at a rough right angle to each other. At the same time, shift your weight to the leg on the active side (the side you're striking with) and lean toward this side slightly with the upper body. Keep the other fist above your jawline for protection. Deliver your fist abruptly to the target (this is a short but powerful technique), as you turn your hip and shift your body weight to the front (toward your opponent). Quickly return the hitting hand to the starting position.

A–C: *Martin demonstrates a front uppercut to the stomach.*
D: *The technique done with the rear arm.*

D

8. Backfist

Targets: Jaw, Temples

Execution:

Start in the fighting position. Move your front fist to your rear shoulder (your palm and fingers should be facing you through the entire movement), and turn the upper body in the same direction. Deliver the fist to the target in a whipping motion, turning the upper body at the same time. Impact is made with the knuckles of the fist, after which the punching hand is quickly returned to the starting position.

A–C: *The backfist to the jaw from a southpaw stance.*
D: *The backfist to the head. This technique is only legal in Semi-Contact.*

A

B

D

C

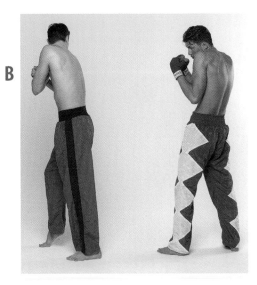

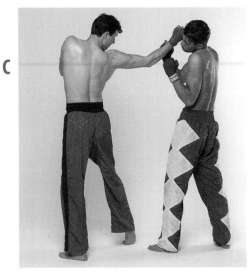

9. Spinning Backfist

Targets: Jaw, Temples

Execution:

From the fighting position, move your front leg forward to the inside and shift your weight onto it. Then, if you've started out in the standard fight stance (left leg forward), you perform a clockwise turn, using the power generated by the rotation to strike your opponent with your rear arm. If you've started out in a southpaw stance, rotate counterclockwise. Either way, contact is made with the knuckles of the rear fist. The turn should be quick—try to get your opponent back in your line of vision as soon as possible—and you should quickly return to the starting position once you've made contact.

This technique is usually delivered with the rear arm; however, if the opponent moves away, the technique can also be delivered with the front arm.

A–C: *The spinning backfist done with the rear arm.*

Kicking Techniques

This chapter introduces frequently used kicking techniques. Note that not all of these techniques are permitted in all versions or by all associations. Low kicks, for example, are not permitted in some matches.

You need not master all techniques to compete; however, the more techniques you can employ, the more difficult it will be for your opponent to figure you out.

Front kick

	1.	Front kick
	2.	Rear Front kick
	3.	Jumping Front kick

Roundhouse kick

	4.	Front Roundhouse kick
	5.	Rear Roundhouse kick
	6.	Jumping Roundhouse kick

Side kick

	7.	Front Side kick
	8.	Rear Side kick
	9.	Jumping Side kick

Back kick

	10.	Back kick
	11.	Jumping Back kick

(box continued)

Crescent kick

12.	Front Crescent kick
13.	Rear Crescent kick
14.	Spinning Crescent kick

Hook kick

15.	Front Hook kick
16.	Rear Hook kick
17.	Spinning Hook kick
18.	Jumping Spinning Hook kick

Ax kick

19.	Front Ax kick
20.	Rear Ax kick

Footsweep

21.	Footsweep in Same Stance
22.	Footsweep in Different Stance

Low kick

23.	Front Low kick
24.	Rear Low kick

A

B

1. Front Kick

> **Targets: Stomach, Solar Plexus, Head**

Execution:

Start off in fighting position. Pull your front knee toward your upper body and point your front foot toward the target. Keep your guard up to defend against your opponent's techniques. Use your hips to push a straight kick into your opponent. Be sure to turn the rear leg slightly to the outside and lean your upper body slightly back (do not lean too far back or you will be off-balance). Impact is made with the ball of the foot, the heel, or with the entire foot. Subsequently, you quickly return the knee to the upper body, before you bring the leg down to the floor.

The front kick is usually carried out with the ball of the foot, as it can be performed quickly enough to stop an opponent's oncoming technique. The heel or the entire foot is used for a powerful offensive front kick.

A–C: *The front kick (using the front leg) to the body.*
D: *The front kick (using the front leg) to the head.*

C

D

A

B

C

2. Rear Front Kick

Targets: Stomach, Solar Plexus, Head

Execution:

Start in fighting position. Pull your rear knee toward your upper body and point your foot toward the target. In the process, turn the rear part of your body forward. Remember to keep your guard up to defend against your opponent's techniques.

Deliver a straight kick with the help of your hips—turn the pivot leg to the outside and lean your upper body slightly back. Impact is made with the ball of the foot, the heel, or the entire foot. Quickly retract the knee toward your chest, before you bring the leg down to the floor.

A–C: *Giovanni shows the rear front kick to the chin.*

3. Jumping Front Kick

Targets: Stomach, Solar Plexus, Head

Execution:

From the fight position, shift your weight to the front leg, bend your front leg slightly, and launch yourself with this leg.

As you jump, pull the rear knee toward your chest and turn the rear part of the body forward. Use the motion of your hips to deliver a straight kick. Impact is made with the ball of the foot, the heel, or the entire foot. Make sure you land properly, with the jumping leg hitting the floor first, and return quickly to the starting position.

This technique can also be performed with the front leg, but it's not as powerful.

A–C: *Andreas shows the jumping front kick with the rear leg.*

A

B

4. Front Roundhouse Kick

Targets: Ribs, Temples, Jaw

Execution:

From the fight position, raise the front leg as you pivot the rear leg to the outside. The knee of your front leg should point toward the target and the leg should be slightly bent. Deliver the kick with a snapping motion, using your hips to generate the power. Impact is made with the instep or the ball of the foot. Subsequently, snap the lower leg back, and return the front leg to the floor.

The front roundhouse kick can be delivered to the body or to the head.

A–C: *Martin demonstrates the kick to the head.*

C

5. Rear Roundhouse Kick

Targets: Ribs, Temples, Jaw

Execution:

From the fight position, raise the rear leg and pivot the front leg toward the outside. The knee of the rear leg should point in the direction of the target and the leg should be slightly bent. When you raise the leg, turn the rear part of the body forward.

Deliver the kick with a snapping motion, using your hips. Impact is made with the instep or the ball of the foot. Subsequently, snap the lower leg back, before returning it to the floor.

The rear roundhouse kick can be delivered to the body or to the head.

A–C: *Martin demonstrates the kick to the body.*

A

B

C

6. Jumping Roundhouse Kick

Targets: Ribs, Temples, Jaw

Execution:

From the fight position, bend your legs slightly and launch yourself with the support leg. As you jump, raise the kicking leg so that the knee is pointing toward the target and the leg is bent. If you perform the technique with the rear leg, you should also simultaneously turn the rear side of the body toward the front.

While you're in the air, kick out the lower leg with a snapping motion, using the support of the hips to generate power. Impact is made with the instep or the ball of the foot. Make sure that you return to the floor properly, with the jumping leg touching down first. Return to the starting position.

This technique can be done with either leg, but the rear leg generates more power.

A–C: *Andreas shows the technique using the front leg.*

7. Front Side Kick

Targets: Stomach, Solar Plexus, Chin, Nose

Execution:

From the fight position, raise your front knee as high as possible in the direction of the opposite shoulder, and point the heel toward your target. At the same time, turn your upper body forward and pivot the rear leg to the back.

Use the support of your hips to deliver the side kick, as you pivot the rear leg further and lean your chest back. Impact is made with the heel or the outside of the foot. At the moment of impact, the heel will be somewhat above the toes. After making contact, you should first pull the leg back toward the shoulder before returning it to the floor. Be sure to keep your guard up as you execute this technique.

A–C: *Martin shows the front side kick to the body.*
D: *Jürgen shows the front side kick to the head.*

A

B

D

C

A

B

8. Rear Side Kick

Targets: Stomach, Solar Plexus, Chin, Nose

Execution:

From the fight position, pull up the rear knee as high as possible toward the opposite shoulder, and point the heel of your foot toward your target. At the same time, turn the rear part of the body and the rear hip toward the front and pivot the front leg toward the back.

Using your hips for support, kick out the leg as you pivot the front leg completely to the back and lean your upper body back. Impact is made with the heel or the outside of the foot. At the moment of impact, the heel will be somewhat above the toes. Pull the knee back to the shoulder, before returning the kicking leg to the floor. Do not drop your guard.

A–C: *Andreas shows the rear side kick to the chin.*

C

9. Jumping Side Kick

Targets: Stomach, Solar Plexus, Chin, Nose

Execution:

Start in the fighting position. Bend your legs slightly and spring up from the support leg. As you jump, pull the knee of the kicking leg toward the opposite shoulder, and turn the upper body and hips toward the front.

Using your hips for support, deliver the kick, making impact with the heel or the outside of the foot. Make sure you land properly balanced, with the jumping leg touching the floor first. Return to your starting position.

A–C: *Martin shows the jumping side kick with the front leg.*
D: *Natalia shows the jumping side kick with the rear leg.*

A

B

D

C

A

B

C

10. Back Kick

Targets: **Stomach, Solar Plexus, Chin, Nose**

Execution:

From the fight position, move one leg laterally toward the inside and shift your body weight onto it. Now turn your back toward your opponent as you pivot the support leg to the outside. From the conventional stance, turn clockwise; from a southpaw position, counterclockwise.

As you turn, pull in the knee of the kicking leg, and deliver the kick with the support of your hips, making contact with the heel or the entire foot. After the rotation, some athletes will initially look at the opponent to gauge distance before kicking, while others can kick instinctively. Remember to pull in the knee before you return the kicking leg to the floor.

This technique is usually carried out with the rear leg, but it can be done with the front leg (e.g. if the opponent is retreating).

A–D: *Martin demonstrates the back kick, turning clockwise.*

D

11. Jumping Back Kick

Targets: Stomach, Solar Plexus, Chin, Nose

Execution:

From the fighting position, move the front leg laterally toward the inside and shift your body weight onto it. Now turn your back toward the opponent—turn clockwise from the conventional stance, counterclockwise from the southpaw stance—and jump while pulling in the rear knee.

Deliver the kick with the raised leg, using your hips for support. After the rotation, some athletes first look at the opponent, while others kick instinctively. Quickly return to a properly balanced starting position, with the jumping leg touching down first.

This technique is usually carried out with the rear leg, but it can be done with the front leg (e.g. if the opponent is retreating).

A–D: *Peter Zaar shows the jumping back kick, using the rear leg.*

A

B

D

C

A

B

C

12. Front Crescent Kick

Targets: **Temples, Jaw**

Execution:

This technique is frequently used to kick away the opponent's guard, which leaves them vulnerable to other strikes. From the fighting stance, turn your rear leg toward the outside and shift your body weight onto it. At the same time, pull the front knee high up in the air.

As you extend the kicking leg, deliver the kick in a semi-circle, with the leg traveling from the inside out to the target. The body and the support leg turn along with the kicking leg—in the direction of the kick. Use your hips to generate power. Impact is made with the outside of the foot. Make sure that you do not drop your guard. After impact, return the kicking leg to the starting position.

A–C: *Giovanni shows the front crescent kick with the front leg.*

13. Rear Crescent Kick

Targets: Temples, Jaw

Execution:

From the fighting position, turn the front leg toward the outside and shift your body weight onto it. At the same time, pull the rear knee high up into the air and pivot the rear side of your body forward.

Deliver the kick in a semi-circle from the inside out to the target as you turn your body and support leg in the direction of the kick. Impact is made with the outside of the foot. Do not drop your guard. Return the leg to the starting position quickly.

A–C: *Martin shows the rear crescent kick.*

A

B

C

D

14. Spinning Crescent Kick

Targets: Temples, Jaw

Execution:

From the fight position, turn your front leg toward the inside front and shift your weight to it. Then, turn clockwise or counterclockwise, depending on which stance you're in (conventional or southpaw). Turn across your front foot and try to regain sight of your opponent as quickly as possible.

As you turn, pull the rear leg high up into the air; in the final phase of the turn, kick in a semi-circular motion from the outside toward the opponent's head, while extending the kicking leg and pivoting on the support leg. Impact is made with the outside of the foot. Return the kicking leg to the starting position quickly.

This technique is usually carried out with the rear leg, but is also possible to use the front leg.

A–D: *Vanessa demonstrates the spinning crescent kick with the rear leg. She turns clockwise.*

15. Front Hook Kick

Targets: Temples, Jaw

Execution:

From the fighting position, pull in your front knee toward the opposite shoulder and slightly raise the lower leg in the process. At the same time, turn your upper body to the front and the support leg to the outside.

Deliver the kick to the opponent's head by extending the leg and moving the lower leg—with the support of the hips—toward the target. The support leg pivots further to the outside as you kick. Impact is made with the heel or the sole of the foot. Remember to bring the kicking leg down first when you return to the starting position.

A–C: *Martin demonstrates the hook kick with the front leg.*

A

B

C

A

16. Rear Hook Kick

Targets: Temples, Jaw

Execution:

From the fighting position, pull your rear knee toward the opposite shoulder, while somewhat raising the lower leg. At the same time, turn the rear side of your body toward the front, and the support leg toward the outside.

Deliver the kick to the opponent's head by extending the leg and using the support of the hips to kick. The support leg turns further toward the outside. Impact is made with the heel or the sole of the foot. Return the kicking leg to the starting position.

A–C: *The rear hook kick.*

B

C

17. Spinning Hook Kick

Targets: Temples, Jaw

Execution:

From the fighting position, move your front leg to the inside and shift your weight onto it. Turn across the front foot—clockwise for the conventional stance, counterclockwise for the southpaw position—and try to regain sight of your opponent at the earliest opportunity.

In the course of the turn, raise your leg and pivot the support leg until the heel of the kicking leg is pointing toward the target. In the final phase, deliver a circular kick from the outside to the opponent's head. Impact is made with the heel or the sole of the foot. Return the kicking leg to the floor and resume the starting position.

This kick can also be carried out with the front leg. To do so, you must move your rear leg toward the inside front and turn across the rear foot. Note that because this version takes slightly longer to execute, it is easier for the opponent to anticipate it and block.

A–D: *Martin shows the hook kick, turning clockwise.*

A

B

C

D

A

B

C

D

18. Jumping Spinning Hook Kick

Targets: **Temples, Jaw**

Execution:

Starting in the fight position, move the front leg forward to the inside and shift your weight onto it. Turn across your front foot—clockwise for right-handers, counterclockwise for southpaws—and try to regain sight of your opponent at the earliest opportunity.

As you turn, jump (springing from your support leg) and raise the kicking leg. In the final phase of the turn, deliver a circular kick from the outside to the opponent's head, while extending the leg and using the support of the hips for greater power. Impact is made with the heel or the sole of the foot. Make sure that you land properly balanced, with the support leg touching down first.

This kick can also be carried out with the front leg. To do so, you must move the rear leg forward to the inside and turn across the rear foot. Note that because this version takes slightly longer to execute, it is easier for the opponent to anticipate it and block.

A–D: *Martin demonstrates a jumping spinning hook kick. He turns clockwise.*

19. Front Ax Kick

Targets: **Center of the Head, Collarbones**

A

Execution:

Start in the fight position, then shift your weight onto the rear leg. Raise your front leg far up (coming from the outside) until it is high above the target. Keep your leg muscles relaxed as you do this, raise the heel of the support leg, and pivot toward the outside.

Deliver a powerful kick from above, tensing the leg muscles in the process. Contact is made with the heel. Make sure that you do not drop your guard as you pull back the leg. After striking your opponent, quickly return to the starting position.

B

A–D: *Vanessa demonstrates the front ax kick to the head. She moves her kicking leg up along Natalia's left side. If you are not as agile as Vanessa, it is recommended that you lift the heel of the pivot leg when it is in the top position.*

D

C

A

20. Rear Ax Kick

Targets: **Center of the Head, Collarbones**

Execution:

From the fight position, shift your weight onto the front leg. Raise your leg high (coming from the inside) until it is well above the target. Remember to keep your leg muscles relaxed, lift the heel of the support leg, and pivot it to the outside. Deliver a powerful kick from above, while tensing the leg muscles. Impact is made with the heel. Make sure not to drop your guard as you return the kicking leg to the floor. Resume the starting position.

A–C: *Vanessa demonstrates the rear ax kick. For this technique, she moves her kicking leg up along Natalia's right side. If you are not as agile as Vanessa, it is recommended that you lift the heel of the pivot leg when it is in the top position.*

B

C

21. Footsweep in Same Stance

A

Targets: **Above the outer ankles**

Execution:

From the fight position, shift your weight onto the front leg. With your rear leg, kick your opponent's foot from the outside: use a circular motion and turn the rear part of the body forward. Impact is made with the inside of the foot, after which you sweep your foot inside and up. Then, retract your foot and resume the starting position.

A–C: *Martin demonstrates the footsweep against an opponent who is in the same stance.*

B

C

A

22. Footsweep in Different Stance

Targets: **Above the outer ankles**

Execution:

From the fight position, shift your weight onto the rear leg, and deliver a circular kick with the front foot from the outside to the opponent's opposite foot (the foot that's closest to your rear foot). Impact is made with the inside of the foot, after which you pull your foot inside and up. Finally, move your foot back and resume the starting position.

A–C: *The footsweep against an opponent who is in a different stance.*

B

C

23. Front Low Kick

Targets: Mid-thigh

Execution:

From the fight position, move your rear leg slightly out and slightly forward, and shift your weight onto it.

Swing the front leg in a semi-circle onto the target, which should be the mid-thigh. To do this kick correctly, you must pivot the support leg to the outside and add the hip motion and your body weight into your kick. Impact is made with the lower end of the shinbone. Pay attention to your guard, as a powerful delivery will leave you vulnerable to the opponent's counter punches. Quickly return your leg to the starting position.

A–C: *The low kick to the inside of the leg. This kick is usually carried out with the shinbone, however, to assess the fight distance, you can also kick with the instep.*

A

B

C

A

B

C

24. Rear Low Kick

Targets: **Mid-thigh**

Execution:

From the fight position, move your front leg slightly to the outside and slightly forward, and shift your weight onto it. Then, deliver the rear low kick in a semi-circle to the target, while keeping the kicking leg mostly straight (i.e., the kick should be one motion, not two). In the process, pivot the support leg to the outside, and add the hip motion and your body weight into the kick. Impact is made with the lower end of the shinbone to the mid-thigh. Pay attention to your guard, as a powerful delivery will leave you vulnerable to the opponent's counter punches. Quickly return your leg to the starting position.

A–C: *Giovanni shows the low kick to the outside of the thigh.*

Part V **Offensive Technique Combinations**

17

Use in Training

Learning combinations enables you to execute a quick sequence of attacking techniques. These are practiced during shadowboxing, on the heavybag, on pads, and with a partner. The combinations must be practiced time and again—in a fight situation you will not have the time to deliberate on which techniques to use and how to combine them with each other. You will use only those techniques and combinations that you have practiced so frequently you are able to perform them instinctively.

In professional kickboxing, once the opponent has been named and his weaknesses and strengths have been analyzed, trainers will have fighters practice combinations and countering tactics. If the opponent, for example, has a powerful straight punch, a kickboxing trainer will repeatedly train the combinations that include offensive kicking techniques to the opponent's punching arm. During the fight, the trainer may provide advice during breaks, pointing out the mistakes of both the athlete and his or her opponent, and advising that the fighter use certain combinations to gain the advantage. It is, however, the fight itself that dictates the use of any techniques.

The following chapter illustrates some frequently used offensive combinations. The abbreviation **l** stands for the left side and **r** for the right side. It is assumed that the reader is using an orthodox stance (right-handed). If you are a southpaw, the moves must be laterally inverted to suit your stance.

18

Sequences of Combinations

Note that because of space constraints, not all of the sequences listed below are pictured.

Combinations of Two Techniques

1. Jab (l), hook (l)

2. Straight punch (r), roundhouse kick to the head (l)

3. Hook (l), spinning hook kick (r)

4. Uppercut (r), roundhouse kick (l)

5. Hook to the body (l), hook to the head (l)

6. Backfist (l), back kick (r)

7. Front kick (l), straight punch (r)

8. Side kick (l), back kick (r)

9. Side kick (l), spinning hook kick (r)

10. Ax kick (l), straight punch (r)

Suggestion 5:

The combination of a hook to the body and a hook to the head (shown here in a southpaw stance). From the starting postion, deliver a hook to the body. Promptly follow up with a hook to the head, for which you use the same arm.

Suggestion 7:

The combination of a front kick and a rear punch (shown here in a southpaw stance). From the starting position, deliver a front kick to the head, using the front leg. Follow it up with a rear straight punch. After the kick, be sure to drop the front leg down to its starting position—don't allow the leg to swing all the way back before returning to the starting position.

Suggestion 8:

The combination of a side kick and a jumping back kick. From the starting position, deliver a side kick to the body with the front leg. Promptly follow up with a jumping back kick, for which you use the rear leg.

Suggestion 9:

The combination of a side kick and a spinning hook kick. From the starting position, deliver a side kick with the front leg. Follow it up with a spinning hook kick, for which you use the rear leg.

Suggestion 10:

The combination of an ax kick and a rear punch. From the starting position, deliver an ax kick with the front leg. Follow it up with a rear straight punch. Make sure that your front leg touches down in the correct position (your fight stance) after completing the ax kick. This way, you will be in position to throw the punch immediately after the kick.

Combinations of Three Techniques

1. Jab (l), straight punch (r), jab (l)

2. Jab (l), side kick (l), spinning hook kick (r)

3. Uppercut (r), hook (l), spinning hook kick (r)

4. Roundhouse kick to the body (l), roundhouse kick to the head (l), straight punch (r)

5. Roundhouse kick (l), straight punch (r), hook (l)

6. Front kick (l), roundhouse kick (r), straight punch (r)

7. Front kick (l), jab (l), low kick (r)

8. Hook kick (l), roundhouse kick (l), straight punch (r)

9. Ax kick (l), straight punch (r), roundhouse kick (r)

10. Ax kick (l), straight punch to the body (r), hook (l)

Suggestion 2:

The combination of a jab, a side kick, and a jumping spinning hook kick. From the starting position, deliver a jab. This is followed up by a side kick with the front leg, and ends with a jumping spinning hook kick, for which you use the rear leg.

Suggestion 4:

The combination of a roundhouse kick to the body, a roundhouse kick to the head, and a rear punch. From the starting position, deliver a fast roundhouse kick to the body with the front leg. Promptly follow up with a roundhouse kick to the head, for which you use the same leg.

Beginners can return the leg to floor between the two kicks, but they should try to touch down only briefly and spring back quickly. Advanced athletes should perform the technique without interruption. After the kicks, drop the front leg down in front; you're your in fighting stance, immediately follow up with a rear straight punch.

Suggestion 10:

The combination of an ax kick, a punch to the body, and a hook. From the starting position, deliver an ax kick with the front leg. Follow up with a rear punch to the stomach and end the combination with a front hook to the head. Be careful not to drop your guard when executing the punch to the stomach.

Combinations of Four Techniques

1) Jab (l), uppercut (r), roundhouse kick (r), jab (l)

2) Jab (l), straight punch (r), jab (l), spinning hook kick (r)

3) Jab (l), hook kick (l), side kick (l), back kick (r)

4) Roundhouse kick (l), jab (l), straight punch (r), roundhouse kick (r)

5) Roundhouse kick (l), straight punch (r), uppercut (l), hook (r)

6) Front kick (l), jab (l), low kick (r), hook (l)

7) Hook kick (l), roundhouse kick (l), straight punch (r), roundhouse kick (r)

8) Crescent kick (l), jab (l), straight punch (r), front kick (r)

9) Crescent kick (l), jab (l), straight punch (r), spinning hook kick (r)

10) Ax kick (l), straight punch (r), uppercut (l), hook (r)

Suggestion 2:

The combination of a jab, a straight punch, another jab, and a spinning hook kick. From the starting position throw a jab, and follow it up with a rear straight punch. Throw another jab, which sets up the spinning hook kick, for which you use the rear leg.

Suggestion 4:

The combination of a roundhouse kick, a jab, a straight punch, and another roundhouse kick. From the starting position, throw a roundhouse kick to the body using your front leg. Follow this with a jab and a rear straight punch. The punches will set up the final move—a rear roundhouse kick to the head.

Suggestion 9:

The combination of a crescent kick, a jab, a straight punch, and a spinning hook kick. From the starting position execute a crescent kick with the front leg. Promptly follow up with a jab and rear straight punch combination. The punches will set up the final move, a spinning hook kick, for which you use the rear leg.

Part VI **Defensive and Countering Techniques**

19

Defense Basics

Now you will learn how to defend against and counter the offensive techniques discussed in the previous chapters.

Kickboxers have two different modes of defense: active and passive. The passive defensive acts against punches and kicks are **blocks, parries, evasive moves,** and **side and back steps**. Passive techniques usually just buy you time to allow you to follow up with a counterattack or a specific combination. Active acts of defense against punches and kicks are **direct counters**, which can be thought of as a blend of defensive and offensive techniques.

It is important to note that if you exclusively concentrate on defense in a contest and not on your own attacking techniques, your opponent will attack you without interruption until he has landed an effective blow.

The fighter attempts to block the opponent's kick by raising his arms.

Blocking

You can interrupt or lessen the impact of an opponent's technique by blocking. The disadvantage to this strategy is that a block always absorbs some of the impact from a technique. For this reason, parries, evasive moves, steps, and direct counters are preferred to blocking as defensive measures. In a contest, however, an opponent's attacks are frequently surprising and quick, so you must learn to block, as it is a technique you will likely have to use.

You can block with the fist, open hand, shoulder, lower arm (right by the elbow), and shinbone.

A: *Blocking a roundhouse kick with the fist. Note that this block is only possible because of the dampening effect of the boxing gloves. It is not meant as a self-defense move.*

B: *Blocking an uppercut with the open hand.*

C: *Blocking a backfist with the lower arm.*

D: *A hook to the body can be blocked with the lower arm.*

E: *Both a roundhouse kick to the body and a low kick can be blocked with the shinbone.*

F & G: *Peter Zaar shows additional ways in which roundhouse kicks and side kicks can be blocked.*

A

Parries

Punches and kicks that come straight from the front, such as the straight punch and the front kick, can be deflected from all directions. The best parries push the punches or kicks to the outside—enough so that your opponent turns and ends up with his back to you. In this position the opponent is unable to use any further attacking techniques, and you can deliver a successful counter. A parry is frequently combined with a step to the outside, which will put you in a position particularly suited for a counterattack.

B

A: *Parry of a rear straight punch to the head. The parry is carried out from left to right.*

B & C: *Parry of a front kick and a side kick to the body. Do not hold the kick: deflect it in a smooth motion to the outside. The parry is often combined with a side step.*

C

Evasive Moves

Evasive moves, such as leaning back, ducking left and right to the front, or ducking down and rolling off to the left or right, can foil an opponent's attack.

A: *Leaning back. Shift your weight to the rear leg and lean back. Make sure to keep your chin tucked toward the chest.*

B: *Ducking left or right is a defense, wherein you move diagonally toward the outside. For example, to defend against a straight right punch, you can duck down and move forward diagonally to the left; the punch should move past your right ear. Against a left straight punch, move diagonally to the right, allowing the punch to slip past your left ear.*

C & D: *Rolling off. You dive just below a hook to the head, straighten up after the punch swings through, and, using the rolling motion of your body, deliver a powerful hook to the body on your way up. Against a left hook you dive to the right and vice versa.*

Side and Back Steps

You can foil an attack with evasive footwork. If you do this correctly, not only will you avoid the blow, but your opponent will end up in an unfavorable position, allowing you to employ an effective counter.

The moves are: back step, side step left, side step right, body turn left with step, and body turn right with step.

A: *Natalia attacks with a kick. Andreas avoids the kick by stepping back. As you step back, you can also lean back slightly.*

B: *You can defend against a front kick or a side kick to the body by taking a step to the side in combination with a parry. To defend against an attack with the left leg, take a step forward to the right, while deflecting the kick with the wrist of the left hand. Reverse this movement to defend against the right leg kick.*

C: *Martin attacks with a high front kick. Peter Zaar takes defensive action, turning his body to the left by pivoting on the front leg and pulling the rear leg along.*

Direct Counter

Once you detect the beginning of your opponent's technique, you can counter with a quicker technique. To this end, you perform a technique in a straight line to the front, (e.g. a straight punch or front kick), or you move away from the opponent's attack sideways and to the front—by doing so you will gain extra time to respond with your own technique (e.g. a hook).

Direct counters require much training and exact timing. They are, however, very effective, as the opponent moves in the direction of the technique, making its impact that much more devastating.

A: *Martin attacks with a jab. Peter Zaar defends with a quick punch to the body.*

B: *Martin starts a roundhouse kick. The direct counter is a quick straight punch to the body.*

Sven Kirsten (left) counters a kick during the 2005 World Championship in Nuremburg, Germany.

20

A Selection of Defensive and Countering Techniques

Generally, defense and counter techniques with the least number of steps are the most likely to succeed. Some kickboxing trainers, however, do teach techniques with many different parts. In theory, the use of such techniques is certainly possible, but you rarely see these used in a real fight. After all, a fighter won't patiently await the conclusion of his opponent's defensive and countering techniques, but will try to interrupt these at the earliest possible occasion.

This book presents a basic repertoire of defensive and countering techniques that athletes can apply in competitive situations. In the course of your athletic career, you should complement this selection with additional techniques; a large number of techniques can be learnt from different trainers, or can be discovered in films or from watching competitions. Keep in mind that each athlete has different physical attributes and skills, which means you'll find some techniques are better suited to you than others. Repeated practice can answer the question of which techniques are most effective for you. A list of many defensive and countering techniques against all possible attacks can be found in the book *Muay Thai: Advanced Thai Kickboxing Techniques* (Delp 2004).

To start out, select three to five techniques and practice them for as long as necessary to become fluent in them. After you've worked on them for some time, start practicing the next set of defensive and countering techniques. This way you'll expand your repertoire of techniques step by step. It makes no sense to practice a large number of techniques for short periods only. They must be practiced again and again in order to perfect delivery and timing. If you do not perfect the techniques, they cannot be used successfully in a fight. The correct moment for the use of a technique may already be over by the time you start to consider using it.

Professional athletes practice defensive and countering techniques in all training sessions. As soon as you learn about your opponent in the next fight, your trainer will develop a training program with techniques tailored to the opponent's characteristics.

Please note

Include defensive and countering techniques in all training sessions. Work on drills with your training partner. Have him or her attack with an agreed upon technique for a few minutes, while you defend and counter using a small set of specific, agreed-upon techniques. To avoid injury, do not deliver any techniques with full power. Do be precise in your movements—the techniques must be carried out correctly or they are often not successful. After a few minutes, switch roles, wherein you become the attacker.

21

Tactics for Countering Punches

1. Deflect a jab to the inside and counter with a hook to the body

2. Duck and punch against a jab

3. Deflect a straight punch to the inside and counter with a roundhouse kick

4. Duck and counter a rear straight punch

5. Lean back to avoid a punch to the body and counter with a backfist

6. Roll under the hook and counter with a hook to the body

7. Block an uppercut and counter with a hook

8. Lower-arm block a hook to the body and counter with an uppercut

9. Block a backfist and counter with a jumping back kick

10. Block a spinning backfist and counter with a side kick

1. Deflect a Jab to the Inside and Counter with a Hook to the Body

Opponent's Technique: **Front straight punch (jab)**

Execution:

Deflect the punch to the inside with the opposite hand as you lean your upper body to the outside. Follow up with a hook to the ribs, using the same arm you used to deflect the punch. Keep your body relaxed, and make sure that you don't deflect the opponent's arm too far to the inside, as such a big motion isn't necessary and it will only slow you down as you try to move in quickly for the hook.

A–D: *Giovanni attacks with a jab. Jürgen deflects the punch to the inside and leans his body slightly back to the outside. He promptly counters with a hook to the ribs, for which he uses the same arm.*

2. Duck and Punch Against a Jab

Opponent's Technique: Front straight punch (jab)

Execution:

Once you detect the beginning of a jab, duck forward to the outside, so that the opponent's punch misses its target. At the same time, deliver a straight punch to the unprotected ribs. If the opponent uses the conventional stance and carries out a punch with the left arm, you quickly duck forward to the right and deliver a left straight punch at the same time. If, however, the opponent is in a southpaw position and delivers a right straight punch, duck forward to the left and deliver a right straight punch at the same time.

A–C: *Andreas (right) attacks with a jab. Peter ducks forward to the right and counters with a jab.*

A

B

C

A

3. Deflect a Straight Punch to the Inside and Counter with a Roundhouse Kick

Opponent's Technique: Rear straight punch, powerful jab

Execution:

Deflect the punch to the inside with the opposite hand and lean your upper body to the outside. Promptly counter with a roundhouse kick to the ribs. Make sure to keep your body relaxed, and don't deflect your opponent's arm too far to the inside, as this will slow your counterattack. This technique can also be used against a powerful jab.

A–D: *Jürgen attacks with a rear straight punch. Giovanni deflects the punch inside to the right and leans toward the outside left. He promptly counters with a rear-leg roundhouse kick to the ribs.*

B

C

D

4. Duck and Counter a Rear Straight Punch

Opponent's Technique: Rear straight punch

Execution:

Once you detect the beginning of a rear straight punch, duck forward to the outside, so that the opponent's punch misses its target. At the same time, deliver a straight punch to the unprotected ribs.

If the opponent uses the conventional stance and carries out his punch with the right arm, duck forward to the left, and promptly deliver a right straight punch. If the opponent uses a southpaw stance and delivers a left straight punch, duck forward to the right, and deliver a left straight punch.

A–C: *Jürgen (left) attacks with a rear straight punch. Martin ducks forward to the left and counters with a rear straight punch.*

D: *If you succeed in hitting the opponent with a hard straight punch, and he is somewhat dazed, you can follow up with a hook kick.*

A

B

C

D

A

5. Lean Back to Avoid a Punch to the Body and Counter with a Backfist

> **Opponent's Technique: Punch to the body (only allowed in Semi-Contact Kickboxing)**

Execution:

In a Semi-Contact match, an opponent may attack with a straight punch to the body. Take a step back and lean back at the same time, so that the punch misses its target. In the process, shift your weight onto the rear leg—you can then jump off the rear leg and counter with a backfist to the head.

A–D: *Peter (left) attacks with a straight punch to the body. Andreas takes a small step back and also leans back. Andreas then counters with a backfist, which is performed while jumping.*

B

C

D

6. Roll Under the Hook and Counter with a Hook to the Body

A

Opponent's Technique: Hook to the head

Execution:

As soon as the opponent starts to throw a hook to the head, move your upper body to the other side and roll under the punch. If the opponent attacks with a right hook, roll under from right to left. If the opponent delivers a left hook instead, roll under from left to right.

As you straighten up, throw a hook into your opponent's ribs.

B

A–C: *Giovanni attacks with a left hook to the head. Jürgen dives below the punch from left to right and delivers a hook to the ribs with the left arm as he rises.*

C

A

7. Block an Uppercut and Counter with a Hook

> **Opponent's Technique: Uppercut to the head**

Execution:

Block the uppercut with the open hand on the same side of the body, so that the other hand can deliver a hook to the unprotected part of the opponent's head. If the opponent attacks with a right uppercut, you block with the right hand and perform the hook with the left. If the opponent attacks with a left uppercut instead, you block with the left hand and deliver the hook with the right.

B

A–C: *Andreas attacks with a right uppercut to the head. Peter blocks the punch with the palm of the right hand. He immediately counters with a left hook to the unprotected side of the head.*

C

8. Lower-Arm Block a Hook to the Body and Counter with an Uppercut

A

Opponent's Technique: Uppercut to the body, hook to the body

Execution:

Your opponent attacks you with an uppercut or hook to the ribs. Block the technique with your opposite lower arm (right above the elbow). Turn the part of your body under attack forward, so that the punch does not hit you with its full strength. Promptly follow up by delivering an uppercut with the other arm to the opponent's chin.

A–C: *Andreas attacks with an uppercut to the ribs. Peter blocks the technique and promptly counters with an uppercut.*

B

C

A

B

9. Block a Backfist and Counter with a Jumping Back Kick

> **Opponent's Technique: Backfist, spinning backfist**

Execution:

Block the oncoming punch with your front forearm. Turn across your front foot—clockwise in a conventional stance, counterclockwise in a southpaw stance—and in the process of turning, jump off the floor with the front leg and pull up the rear knee. Deliver a kick with the raised leg to the opponent's body. Make sure you land properly, with the jumping leg touching down first. Resume the fight position.

As an alternative you can also deliver a side kick with the front leg to the opponent's body.

A–D: *Jürgen (left) attacks with a backfist. Martin blocks the attack with the front arm, turns clockwise, and carries out a jumping back kick.*

C

D

10. Block a Spinning Backfist and Counter with a Side Kick

A

Opponent's Technique: Spinning backfist, backfist

Execution:

Block the oncoming punch with your front forearm, and move the blocking arm slightly forward as you do so in order to rob your opponent's attack of its full power. Now carry out a side kick with the front leg to your opponent's unprotected body.

This technique can be carried out from both conventional and southpaw stances.

A–D: *Peter (left) attacks with a spinning backfist while turning counterclockwise. Andreas blocks the attack with the front arm and promptly counters with a side kick to the body.*

B

D

C

🦶 **Countering a kick with a hook kick.**

22

Tactics for Countering Kicks

1. Deflect a front kick or side kick and counter with a straight punch

2. Block a front kick and counter with a spinning hook kick

3. Use a spinning hook kick against a roundhouse kick

4. Fist block a high roundhouse kick and counter with a body punch

5. Evade the hook kick and counter with a hook to the body

6. Lean back to avoid a spinning hook kick and counter with a hook kick

7. Pull up the knee to avoid a footsweep and counter with a side kick

8. Sidestep an ax kick and counter with a straight punch

9. Block a low kick to the outside and counter with a roundhouse kick

10. Retract the leg to avoid a low kick to the inside and counter with a roundhouse kick

A

1. Deflect a Front Kick or Side Kick and Counter with a Straight Punch

> **Opponent's Technique: Front kick to the body, side kick to the body**

Execution:

Take a step forward to the outside and, at the same time, deflect the kick to the side. If the opponent attacks with the left leg, take a step with the right leg to the right and deflect the technique with the left hand, sweeping the kick to the left. If the opponent uses the right leg, take a step forward to the left and deflect the kick with the right hand, sweeping the kick to the right.

Depending on the fighting distance, you can counter with a straight punch or a roundhouse kick.

A–D: *Martin performs a front kick with the left leg. Peter takes a step forward to the right and deflects the technique to the inside. He then counters with a straight punch to the head.*

B

C

D

2. Block a Front Kick and Counter with a Spinning Hook Kick

Opponent's Technique: Front kick

Execution:

When your opponent attacks with a front kick of the front leg, punch his or her foot to the outside with the front forearm and quickly turn across the front foot—clockwise from a conventional stance, counterclockwise from a southpaw stance. As you turn, raise the rear leg and deliver a hook kick in the final phase of the rotation. Afterwards, return the kicking leg to the floor and resume the fighting stance.

A–D: *Jürgen (left) attacks with a front kick. Martin pushes the technique down to the right side and promptly follows up with a spinning hook kick (turning clockwise).*

A

B

D

C

A

3. Use a Spinning Hook Kick against a Roundhouse Kick

| Opponent's Technique: **Roundhouse kick** |

Execution:

Once you detect the beginning of your opponent's roundhouse kick, quickly turn across the front foot—clockwise from the conventional stance, counter-clockwise from the southpaw position. As you turn, raise the rear leg and carry out a hook kick in the final phase of the rotation. Return the kicking leg to the floor and resume the fight position.

As an alternative you can also counter with a back kick.

A–D: *Jürgen (left) begins a roundhouse kick. Giovanni detects the start of the technique and promptly counters with a spinning hook kick from a clockwise turn.*

B

C

D

4. Fist Block a High Roundhouse Kick and Counter with a Body Punch

> **Opponent's Technique: Roundhouse kick to the head**

A

Execution:

Block your opponent's kick with the fist on the side of your body that's being attacked. To avoid injury, block the kick at the ankle joint, not at the shinbone. As the opponent retracts his leg to the starting position, you can counter with a straight punch to the stomach.

B

If the opponent attacks the rear side of your body, block with the rear fist and deliver your counter with the front fist. When countering, take a small step forward to add more power to the punch.

A–D: *Andreas attacks with a high roundhouse kick. Peter blocks the technique with the left fist. He then counters with a straight punch to the body.*

C

D

5. Evade the Hook Kick and Counter with a Hook to the Body

> **Opponent's Technique: Hook kick, spinning hook kick**

Execution:

Once you detect the beginning of an opponent's hook kick, take a step forward to the outside for protection. If the opponent kicks with the right leg, take a step forward to the left; if he uses the left leg, take a step forward to the right. Make sure that you guard your head with the hand opposite the kick. As the opponent retracts his or her leg, counter with a body hook to the unprotected ribs.

A–C: *Natalia delivers a hook kick with the right leg. Vanessa takes a small step forward to the left, so that the attack misses its target. As soon as Natalia retracts the leg, Vanessa counters with a body hook to the ribs. If Natalia were to kick with the left leg, Vanessa would have to take a forward step to the right and change her stance in the process.*

6. Lean Back to Avoid a Spinning Hook Kick and Counter with a Hook Kick

A

Opponent's Technique: Spinning hook kick, hook kick, spinning crescent kick

Execution:

Lean back with the upper part of your body, so that the opponent's attack misses its target. You must shift your weight to the rear leg to do so. Make sure to tuck your chin toward the chest to protect your throat. You may take a step backward if you need the extra distance to safely evade the technique.

B

You can counter this evasive tactic with a hook kick to the head.

A–D: *Peter attacks with a spinning hook kick from a clockwise rotation. Andreas leans back, so that the attack misses its target. He then counters promptly with a front hook kick.*

C

D

A

7. Pull Up the Knee to Avoid a Footsweep and Counter with a Side Kick

> **Opponent's Technique: Footsweep**

Execution:

Lift the knee of the leg being attacked just enough for the opponent to miss his or her target. As you do so, turn the upper body and the hip forward and pivot the support leg toward the rear. From this position, you can quickly counter with a side kick without having to lower your leg first.

A–C: *Peter carries out a footsweep with the left leg. Andreas pulls up his right knee and promptly counters with a side kick.*

B

C

8. Sidestep an Ax Kick and Counter with a Straight Punch

Opponent's Technique: Ax kick, crescent kick, high front kick

Execution:

Once you detect the beginning of an opponent's ax kick, take a step forward to the outside for protection. If the opponent kicks with the right leg, step to the left; if he uses the left leg, step to the right. Make sure you guard your head with the hand closest to the kick. While the opponent retracts his leg, you can counter with a powerful straight front punch.

A–C: *Andreas (right) delivers an ax kick with the front leg. Peter takes a quick step forward to the right, for which he changes his stance. Peter promptly counters with a straight punch. If Andreas kicks with the right leg, Peter must take a step forward to the left, which does not require him to change his stance.*

A

B

C

D

9. Block a Low Kick to the Outside and Counter with a Roundhouse Kick

Opponent's Technique: Low kick to the outside

Execution:

Block the opponent's kick with the opposite shinbone, while keeping the support leg extended. Raise the blocking leg in accordance with the level of the opponent's kick. In the event of a kick to the body, raise your leg all the way up to your elbow. After the block, briefly touch your foot to the floor and then promptly counter with a roundhouse kick to the opponent's head or body, using the same leg.

This technique can also be used to block a kick to the inside of the leg; however, the counter will be considerably more difficult to carry out.

A–D: *Jürgen (left) attacks with a low kick. Giovanni blocks the technique with the opposite leg, briefly touches his leg to the floor, and carries out a roundhouse kick.*

10. Retract the Leg to Avoid a Low Kick to the Inside and Counter with a Roundhouse Kick

> **Opponent's Technique: Low kick to the inside**

A

Execution:

The opponent delivers a low kick to the inside of your front leg. Retract the leg that's under attack in a semi-circle movement, so that the opponent's kick misses its target. To best set up the counter kick, perform a sweeping turn with your upper body. Counter with a roundhouse kick, using your rear leg.

Note that countering with a low kick to the outside of the leg is risky, as it may give your opponent a chance to hit your support leg.

B

A–D: *Jürgen (left) attacks with a low kick to the inside of the leg. Giovanni pulls his leg back and counters with a roundhouse kick.*

D

C

Part VII
Feinting

23

Basics

Fighters use feints to mislead their opponents, tempting them to neglect their protective stances. A feint is a phantom technique: you appear
to be carrying out a technique to a certain part of the body—a feint
may entail light contact—but really you are just distracting your opponent, while setting up a more powerful technique. They may drop their
guard or neglect to protect another part of the body while they are
attending to your feint, which means they will then be wide open for
a subsequent technique.

A feint must be carried out quickly and the body must be relaxed.
A slow feint enables the opponent to launch a powerful counterattack,
thus stopping you from executing your follow-up technique. Note that
because it is not essential to make contact, feints are not necessarily carried out within a complete sequence of moves.

You should always throw a feint at a level different than the follow-
up technique. The aim is make your opponent change his or her guard,
allowing you to deliver the follow-up technique to an unprotected part
of the body. So, if you feint to the head, follow up with a technique
to the body. Be careful to eye the target of the feint and not the actual
target of the follow-up technique, or you may betray your motives to
your opponent.

Not all feints are suited for all kickboxers. Some athletes find it difficult to carry out feints. Do a test run of the following feints and select the techniques you are best able to perform. Practice these feints in the next weeks and months until their execution becomes automatic. Then try another set of feints, building your repertoire step by step. The more feints you master, the more difficult it is for the opponent to figure you out; however, feints are only successful if they are performed to perfection. Therefore, even previously acquired feints must be trained again and again in order to perfect their execution and timing in competition.

24

The Best Feints

1. Feint: front kick
   Follow-up technique: jab

2. Feint: front kick
   Follow-up technique: hook kick with the same leg

3. Feint: front kick
   Follow-up technique: roundhouse kick with the same leg

4. Feint: hook
   Follow-up technique: back kick

5. Feint: roundhouse kick to the body
   Follow-up technique: roundhouse kick to the head

6. Feint: roundhouse kick to the body
   Follow-up technique: hook kick with the same leg

7. Feint: side kick
   Follow-up technique: rear straight punch

8. Feint: side kick to the body
   Follow-up technique: side kick to the head

9. Feint: side kick to the body
   Follow-up technique: backfist

10. Feint: footsweep
    Follow-up technique: roundhouse kick with the other leg

11. Feint: opening up the guard in the same stance
    Follow-up technique: rear straight punch

12. Feint: opening up the guard in a different stance
    Follow-up technique: rear straight punch

A

B

C

1. Feint: Front Kick

Follow-up Technique: **Jab**

Execution:

From the fight position, you feint a front kick to the body by raising the front leg. Instead of delivering a powerful kick, you quickly lower the leg back to the floor in front of you and throw a jab. Shift your weight to the front leg for a more powerful punch.

This feint must be done quickly, so that the opponent is caught by surprise and lowers his or her guard, allowing your jab to get through unimpeded.

A–C: *Giovanni feints a front kick to the body by pulling up the front knee. Martin reacts and lowers his guard somewhat to protect his body. Giovanni quickly returns the leg to the floor in front of him and delivers a powerful jab to Martin's unguarded head.*

2. Feint: Front Kick

Follow-up Technique: Hook kick with the same leg

Execution:

Feint a front kick to the body with your front leg, but do not return it to the floor. Instead, pivot and deliver a hook kick to the unprotected head.

This feint requires quickness—you want to land the hook kick while your opponent has lowered his or her arms to protect his or her midsection.

A–C: *Martin feints a front kick to the body. Giovanni lowers his guard slightly for protection. Martin promptly retracts the kicking leg a little and carries out a hook kick to the head.*

A

3. Feint: Front Kick

Follow-up Technique: Roundhouse kick with the same leg

Execution:

Feint a front kick to the body with the front leg. Instead of completing the kick to the body, pull up the leg while in motion, pivot, and deliver a roundhouse kick to the unprotected head.

Again, the aim is to make the opponent lower his or her arms to protect the midsection, while you quickly deliver the kick to the head.

A–C: *Martin feints a front kick to the body. Jürgen lowers the guard slightly for protection. Martin now promptly continues with a roundhouse kick to the head.*

B

C

4. Feint: Hook

Follow-up Technique: Back kick

Execution:

Surprise the opponent with a quick hook. You're not trying to land the blow—just throw it out into the air to deceive your opponent. If the feint succeeds and the opponent moves back or pulls up his guard, you can use the momentum of the punch for a quick rotation. You then deliver a back kick to the unprotected body.

Feinting a left hook, you turn clockwise and perform the back kick with the right leg. For a right hook, turn counterclockwise and kick with the left leg.

A–C: *Martin feints a right hook. Giovanni leans his upper body back for defense. Martin then rotates counterclockwise and continues with a back kick to the body, for which he uses the left leg.*

A

B

C

A

5. Feint: Roundhouse Kick to the Body

> **Follow-up Technique: Roundhouse kick to the head**

Execution:

From the fight position, throw a quick roundhouse kick to the body, making light contact. Retract the lower leg in a snapping motion, but do not return it to the floor—continue the move with a powerful kick to the opponent's head. In the process, the hips are completely turned in and the pivot leg is turned to the rear. This dual technique is usually carried out from the front side of the body, but is also possible from the rear side.

If you do this technique quickly, your opponent will lower his or her the guard to block the body kick with his or her arms.

A–C: *Giovanni shows the feint to the body and performs a powerful roundhouse kick to the head.*

B

C

6. Feint: Roundhouse Kick to the Body

> **Follow-up Technique: Hook kick with the same leg**

Execution:

From the fight position, deliver a swift roundhouse kick to the opponent's ribs, making light contact. Promptly retract the leg a little—do not return it to the floor—and perform a hook kick to the unprotected head.

Your opponent will lower his or her arms to block the body kick. You must quickly execute the kick to the head before they resume their guard.

A–B: *Giovanni delivers a quick roundhouse kick to the left side of the body, so that Martin lowers the guard to the left. Giovanni promptly continues with a hook kick to the right side of the head, using the same leg.*

A

7. Feint: Side Kick

Follow-up Technique: **Rear straight punch**

Execution:

From the fight position, feint a side kick or a round-house kick at body level, by pulling up the front knee and slightly turning the upper body to the side. Instead of carrying out the kick, promptly return the leg to the floor in front of you and continue with a powerful straight punch of the rear arm to the unprotected head.

Execute this technique quickly, so that your opponent is caught by surprise, and responds by lowering his or her arms for protection.

A–C: *Jürgen feints a kick with the front leg. He then continues with a powerful straight punch of the rear arm to the opponent's head.*

B

C

8. Feint: Side Kick to the Body

Follow-up Technique: Side kick to the head

Execution:

From the fight position, feint a side kick to the body by quickly pulling up the knee and delivering a kick to the opponent's body. You then retract the leg, leaving it up in the air, and follow-up with a powerful side kick to the unprotected head.

Do not leave your leg in the air for long—this feint requires quick execution. The opponent may lower the arm to block the body kick, leaving him or her open for the head kick. Note that you may make slight contact with the target with the feint, or you can retract the leg before contact. Only the technique to the head is delivered with full power.

As an alternative, you can also feint a side kick to the head, so that the opponent pulls his guard up. You then perform a side kick to the unprotected part of the body.

A–C: *Martin feints a side kick to the body. He then retracts the leg, and carries out a powerful side kick to the head.*

A

9. Feint: Side Kick to the Body

Follow-up Technique: **Backfist**

Execution:

From the fight position, feint a side kick to the body by quickly pulling up the knee and making light contact to the opponent's body. You then return the leg to the floor in front of you, and at the same time, deliver a powerful backfist, for which you must shift your weight in the opponent's direction.

Be sure to do this move quickly, so that you catch your opponent by surprise, causing him or her to lower the arms for protection. The feint can make light contact with the target, or you can retract the leg before contact is made. Only the backfist is thrown with full power.

B

A–C: *Martin feints a left side kick to the body. As his leg touches the floor, he carries out a left backfist.*

C

10. Feint: Footsweep

Follow-up Technique: Roundhouse kick with the other leg

Execution:

Carry out a quick footsweep, so that the opponent loses his balance a bit, making it difficult for him to defend himself. Do not follow through with the sweep or exaggerate the motion too much. You must swiftly return the leg to the floor, and carry out a roundhouse kick to the body with the other leg.

Don't let the footsweep slow you down, but make sure it affects the opponent enough for him to lose his balance slightly.

A–C: *Martin starts a fast footsweep with the rear leg. He quickly retracts the leg and delivers a powerful roundhouse kick to the body with his front leg.*

A

B

C

A

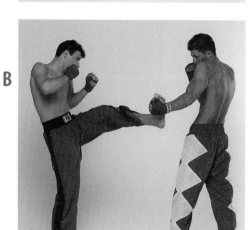

B

C

11. Feint: Opening Up the Guard in the Same Stance

> **Follow-up Technique: Rear straight punch**

Execution:

Your opponent and you share the same stance. Use the front leg to kick the opponent's lead hand in a circular motion from inside out—this will open up his or her guard. (Impact is made with the inside of the foot.) Promptly follow up with a powerful straight punch to your opponent's unprotected head.

Make sure you don't drop your guard during the feint or the follow-up.

A–C: *Martin uses his front leg to kick Giovanni's leading hand and open his guard. Martin swiftly continues with a straight punch of the rear arm.*

12. Feint: Opening Up the Guard in a Different Stance

Follow-up Technique: Rear straight punch

Execution:

Your stance is different than that of your opponent. Use your front leg to kick the opponent's leading hand in a circular motion inside out to open the guard. (Impact is made with the outside of the foot.) You swiftly continue with a powerful straight punch with the rear arm to the unprotected head. Make sure to keep your guard up.

A–C: *Giovanni fights in a conventional stance. Martin has adopted a southpaw position. Giovanni uses his front leg to kick Martin's hand inside out and swiftly continues with a rear straight punch.*

A

B

C

Part VIII
Training

25

The Training Plan

Kickboxers have to train many years to acquire the lightning-speed punching techniques and spectacular kicks that thrill us in the ring. You, too, can develop such extraordinary skills, but only if you continually practice all core areas of kickboxing, as described in this book.

There are three phases to training: the warm-up, the main workout, and the cool-down. Warming up helps prepare your body for intensive training, and includes some exercises to literally warm up the body, followed by exercises to stretch the muscles.

In the main training section, you learn individual techniques and how to use them in combinations. These are trained in shadowboxing, in partner drills, and on equipment, such as punching bags and pads. Advanced athletes also practice by sparring.

The cool-down phase normally starts off with some exercises to strengthen the muscles. Concentrate on the abdominal and lower-back muscles, and on other groups of muscles neglected in previous training sessions. This phase can also include some self-defense exercises. The training session is concluded with some stretching exercises, which help to gently cool down the muscles to avoid cramping, and to assist in a quick regeneration of the body.

Sample training session

1. Warm-up		
	1.1 Warm-up exercise	Time: 10 min
	1.2 Stretching	Time: 15 min
2. Main section		Time: 50 min
	Shadowboxing	
	Technique training with partner	
	Heavybag training and pad training	
	Sparring	
3. Cool-down		
	3.1 Muscle strengthening	Time: 5 min
	(abdominal and lower-back muscles)	
	3.2 Cool-down exercise	Time: 5 min
	3.3 Stretching	Time: 5 min

Note: Self-defense exercises can also be added to the cool-down phase.
The entire training session is 90 minutes.

The recommended time periods in the above chart are simply suggestions. Each kickboxing trainer develops his own program. However, it should be somewhat similar to the following program, to ensure that it comprises all of the important elements of kickboxing training.

If you train on your own, you should adapt the following suggestions to your own requirements and performance level. If, for example, you are aiming for greater agility, you can intensify the stretching program. Or, if you do not have a partner, you can extend the shadowboxing and heavybag training sections. The muscle-strengthening workout can be omitted if you regularly build your muscles in other training sessions. Regardless of how you tailor your program, during each training session you must warm up, stretch, and cool down.

26

Warm-up

The warm-up phase prepares your body for training, making you less susceptible to injuries. The initial warm-up is always followed by stretching.

Warm-up exercise

Start with an activity that warms up your body and prepares it for training. Select an exercise that can be carried out at a constant pace. You should feel comfortable—do not overexert yourself or carry out any quick or jerky movements. This phase is meant to prepare your body for training, not for performance. Choose a level of intensity at which you are still just able to hold a conversation, and exercise for five to ten minutes, or until your body produces its first drops of sweat.

Slow jogging and skipping rope are well suited for the warm-up. In the early phase of skipping, you should not do any high or difficult skips (e.g. double skips), to avoid injury. "Boxing on the spot" is also suitable for the warm-up. Stand with the legs shoulder-width

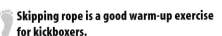 **Skipping rope is a good warm-up exercise for kickboxers.**

apart, and practice uppercuts and head-level punches without interruption for five to ten minutes. Bend your knees somewhat to facilitate the punches, but do not leave the standing position (i.e., do not practice your footwork at this time).

Stretching

Now that you've warmed up your body, you can stretch safely. Stretch all of your muscles, particularly the weaker ones. Stretching lessens muscle tension, making the body more flexible. If you don't stretch, you risk injury when carrying out kickboxing techniques.

Stretch as often as you like, especially if you notice any tension in your muscles. Stretching exercises must be carried out regularly. After some months, and with many stretching exercises, you will be able to perform "extreme" moves, such as high kicks.

For the stretching program, you should plan a period of at least fifteen minutes. However, if agility is the main aim of your training session, you can extend this phase at will.

High-kicking techniques require intensive stretching as preparation.

27

Main Section

In the main section, you learn offensive techniques, combinations, and defensive and countering techniques. The section includes shadowboxing, partner drills, and training on heavybags and pads. You must first study the techniques by shadowboxing into the air, after which you can deliver these against an object. Advanced students add sparring to their training sessions.

Shadowboxing

In shadowboxing, you practice your techniques into the air. Deliver the techniques swiftly, but not with full power or to completion, to protect your joints.

Beginners initially practice individual techniques slowly and gradually build up speed; once they're proficient in the individual techniques, they can practice them in combinations. The trainer closely monitors these steps, so that the athlete does not get into bad habits. Many athletes, for example, tend to drop their guard when executing swift combinations. (When learning on your own, you should practice the techniques in front of a mirror and monitor their execution with the help of this book.)

Advanced students perfect their shadowboxing by acting as if they have a real opponent in front of them. They move toward him, step away, and escape to the side. In the process, they use their entire repertoire of techniques, defending themselves against the techniques of their imaginary opponent, and carrying out counterattacks.

In *preparation for a fight,* the shadowboxing routine will be tailored to the future opponent. The athlete imagines the typical style of his opponent and practices his own tactics in shadowboxing.

Technique Training with a Partner

Offensive, defensive, and countering techniques can be practiced (gently) on an individual to better develop a feel for timing and distance. The techniques used are agreed upon ahead of time and carried out with a lot of control and very little power.

Beginners initially practice individual techniques. The attacking athlete may, for example, deliver a jab, which the defending athlete deflects to the inside and counters with a punch. The technique is repeated for several minutes, after which the training partners switch roles. Once both partners have had a chance to practice the technique, the next technique is announced and practiced in a similar manner.

In this way, the first months of training cover a basic selection of defensive and countering techniques.

Advanced students repeat some techniques in each training session in order to perfect them, but they also keep on adding new techniques to expand their repertoires. Additionally, "free" partner training is an option: one of the two athletes only uses offensive techniques, while the other only uses defensive and countering techniques. It is of great importance that the attacking techniques are carried out with great control and precision, but with little strength; otherwise, the defending athlete may become tense and only use a small range of techniques that he knows particularly well.

In *competitive training,* particular emphasis is attached to the training of defensive and countering techniques that will be most effective against the next opponent. If it is known, for example, that the opponent is an aggressive fighter, special importance will be given to the training of blocking and deflection techniques.

Pad Training

In pad training, the techniques are practiced on pads, focus mitts, and kicking shields to develop a feel for timing and distance. You may deliver the techniques at full strength, unless the pad holder requests otherwise. This may frequently happen, if the trainer is considerably lighter than the athlete, or if the pads are very thin. You must then practice with less power, concentrating more on the correct execution of techniques.

For a *beginner* it is necessary to determine the exact technique prior to this type of training. The trainer calls the name of the technique and holds the pads accordingly. The athlete must only carry out that technique; otherwise, the risk of injury to the trainer or athlete due to an incorrect delivery will be too high. The techniques are initially carried out individually and are combined at a later stage. One combination is frequently repeated for the duration of one round (three minutes) before another combination is reviewed and practiced.

Advanced students can carry out a "free" training, that is, the trainer moves the pads into a position to which the student instinctively delivers an appropriate technique. In the course of training, the trainer points out the athlete's mistakes. He may, for example, deliver a light hook with the pad to the unprotected part of the head to let the athlete know he has dropped his guard.

Pad training is of particular importance in *fight preparation*, as the trainer is in the position to simulate different situations and styles. He may, for example, apply pressure to the athlete by moving toward him, demanding to be stopped by front kicks and side kicks. He can also use attacking techniques for teaching counters. This way, he is able to teach a fight pattern that has been tailored to the athlete's next opponent.

Heavybag Training

Heavybag training helps harden the body, and helps develop power and stamina. You should, therefore, try to deliver each punch and kick with the greatest possible strength. Make sure your execution is technically precise. To avoid injuries when practicing punching techniques, make sure to keep your wrist straight and firm.

Beginners practice combinations of techniques, at first slowly and then swiftly. The trainer prescribes the combinations and monitors the athlete so that he or she does not develop bad habits.

Advanced students can practice freely on a heavybag, that is, they practice without any prescribed combinations, but punch and kick on

instinct. The trainer watches his student and issues instructions, (for example, the more frequent use of high roundhouse kicks), or he demands the use of certain sequences to effect changes to the athlete's fighting pattern.

In *preparation for a fight,* the trainer determines some combinations that are tailored to the style of the next opponent. The student must then practice these sequences again and again, so that he is able to use these instinctively in competition.

Sparring

Sparring is used for the free practice of offensive, defensive, and countering techniques; the techniques have not been agreed upon beforehand. This is supposed to simulate a real fight situation; however, do not deliver the techniques at full strength, as this may injure your training partner. You must cooperate, so that you both improve.

Only *advanced students* may practice sparring. A trainer, who will communicate mistakes, must monitor the athletes; he will determine which weapons may be used. Frequently, for example, only box sparring will be carried out to train fighters to keep their guard up at all times. The trainer may also direct the athletes not to use their preferred or best techniques. This way, the athletes are forced to practice the application of other techniques and enlarge their technical repertoire.

For *competitive training,* a partner will be selected who has the most similarities to the next opponent in terms of stature, style, and preferred techniques. The partner tries to copy the opponent's style. The athlete must then react in accordance with a fight pattern determined by his trainer.

Cool-down

The cool-down phase in training starts with some strengthening exercises, after which some trainers add in self-defense exercises. The training session is concluded by cooling down the body and stretching the muscles.

Muscle-Strengthening Workout

The following strengthening exercises are used in many gyms during the cool-down phase.

A: Crunch. Raise and lower the upper body at a steady, smooth pace by contracting the stomach muscles; do not jerk around or raise yourself by pulling on your neck. Do not sit all the way up: the crunch is held at the midway mark, so that the stomach muscles remain tense throughout the entire exercise.

B: Beetle. You raise the upper body to one side. In the process, the knee on the other side of the body is pulled up and a grip is applied to the inside of the foot. Subsequently, the exercise is carried out to the other side.

C: Superman. Lie flat on your stomach with your arms stretched out in front of you. Lift the left arm, the head, and the right leg, and hold this position for a few seconds. Subse-

quently, the exercise is carried out with the right arm and the left leg. As a variant, you can simultaneously raise both arms and both legs.

Muscle Workout

You may either schedule muscle-strengthening sessions on days you don't train kickboxing, or integrate some exercises into the cool-down phase of your kickboxing regimen.

If you add strengthening exercises to your kickboxing training, you should practice in accordance with the power-stamina method, which dictates 15–30 repetitions per set. Muscle building exercises should be practiced in separate training sessions.

Strengthening exercises done after the main kickboxing phase should preferably be those that strengthen the muscles of the upper and lower back, the central and rear parts of the shoulders, and the abdominals.

Cool-down Exercise

To relax the muscles, you should cool down after the main training phase. This will also help the body regenerate more quickly. The moves should be carried out at slow pace for approximately five minutes, without physical exertion. Slow jogging or cycling at low intensity are particularly suitable cool-down exercises.

Stretching

When you finish training, you should stretch once more. Do not use any extreme or deep stretch positions, as the muscles will be tired and prone to cramping. Stretching at the end of training relaxes tense muscles and prevents them from cramping or shortening.

29

Training Program for Beginners

Your performance will quickly improve if you commit to three kickboxing sessions per week plus extra fitness training. Fitness training provides better staying power, which facilitates longer sport-specific training and puts more power behind your techniques.

You must frequently amend your training plans to the new demands of your body. If your body gets too accustomed to the training, your progress will stagnate. Therefore, you should introduce new training cycles every 6–12 weeks, with each having somewhat different aims. It is recommended that you keep a log of your training plans and performance, so that you are able to monitor your long-term development. Further information on fitness training may be gathered from the book *Fitness for Full-Contact Fighters* (Delp 2006).

The 10-week Program

This sample ten-week program can be used to improve your conditioning in order to obtain better results in kickboxing. The first few weeks' objective is to improve your basic stamina. The subsequent weeks ensure that the stamina is maintained and power training is intensified.

Weeks 1–6 are dedicated to improving kickboxing performance, for which three weekly sessions have been allocated. Additionally, basic stamina will be improved with two fitness sessions. You'll also get accustomed to power training by adding one session per week.

The intensity of the kickboxing sessions is maintained throughout *weeks 7–10*. At this time, the foremost aim in stamina training is to maintain your performance level, for which one session per week is sufficient. Power training is increased to two sessions per week.

S = Stamina. The session is dedicated to stamina-building activities, like jogging.

K = Kickboxing. The session is dedicated to kickboxing. The training also boosts agility, thanks to the extensive stretching program in the warm-up phase. Cardio is improved through intensive training. Furthermore, physical strength is improved, and you can opt to add some power exercises to the end of the session.

M = Muscles. The session is dedicated to power training. It is recommended to use a whole-body program with dumbbells and/or power equipment, as outlined in Program A.

Break. A rest day is required to give the body a chance to regenerate.

	Day 1	Day 2	Day 3	Day 4	Day 5	Day 6	Day 7
Week 1	K	S	K	M	K	S	Break
Week 2	K	S	K	M	K	S	Break
Week 3	K	S	K	M	K	S	Break
Week 4	K	S	K	M	K	S	Break
Week 5	K	S	K	M	K	S	Break
Week 6	K	S	K	M	K	S	Break
Week 7	K	M	K	S	K	M	Break
Week 8	K	M	K	S	K	M	Break
Week 9	K	M	K	S	K	M	Break
Week 10	K	M	K	S	K	M	Break

30

Training Program for Advanced Athletes

Advanced athletes train in accordance with individual training programs tailored to their requirements, for example, in preparation of the next fight. Professional kickboxing athletes usually prepare themselves for a contest with a training program covering 8–12 weeks. Once the opponent and framework conditions for the fight have been determined, the trainer develops a program, in which the weight to be lost and the fight style of the opponent are taken into consideration. In periods without competitive fights, the training cycles aim to eliminate the kickboxer's weak points. The program can also be dedicated primarily to the reduction of body fat or to the build-up of muscles, so that the kickboxer can compete in a more suitable weight division.

As a rule, kickboxing athletes should divide their training in cycles of 6–12 weeks. This requires exact planning of minutes of the training, as it becomes progressively more difficult to improve the performance. The body must constantly receive new intensive challenges, as this is the only way to achieve further improvement. You must always include training specific to kickboxing, stamina training at different levels of intensity, and power training for all muscle groups. Even though the programs determine different priorities, the aim must be to maintain the performance level in those areas that are not the priority of training. This means for fitness training that a minimum of one training session per week must be dedicated to stamina and one session to power with a whole-body program.

Training Program: Performance Improvement

This intensive program primarily serves to improve the kickboxing performance. Preconditions for the success of the program are a healthy diet in accordance with your requirements, and sufficient rest time for regeneration. The program covers six weeks, after which the intensity is somewhat reduced and a new training program takes over.

Day 1. A stamina training session (S) in the morning (e.g. 40–60 minutes of jogging), kickboxing training in the afternoon.

Day 2. Dedicated to kickboxing (K) training.

Day 3. Dedicated to kickboxing (K) training, with sparring being the priority.

Day 4. An intensive power (M) training session. This will be a whole-body program (see pp. 210–214).

Day 5. Stamina (S) training in the morning (e.g. 40–60 minutes of jogging), kickboxing (K) in the afternoon.

Day 6. Dedicated to kickboxing (K) training, with sparring being the priority.

Day 7. A day of rest to aid the body's regeneration.

	Day 1	Day 2	Day 3	Day 4	Day 5	Day 6	Day 7
Week 1	S (TS 1) + K (TS 2)	K	K Sparring	M	S (TS 1) + K (TS 2)	K Sparring	Break
Week 2	S (TS 1) + K (TS 2)	K	K Sparring	M	S (TS 1) + K (TS 2)	K Sparring	Break
Week 3	S (TS 1) + K (TS 2)	K	K Sparring	M	S (TS 1) + K (TS 2)	K Sparring	Break
Week 4	S (TS 1) + K (TS 2)	K	K Sparring	M	S (TS 1) + K (TS 2)	K Sparring	Break
Week 5	S (TS 1) + K (TS 2)	K	K Sparring	M	S (TS 1) + K (TS 2)	K Sparring	Break
Week 6	S (TS 1) + K (TS 2)	K	K Sparring	M	S (TS 1) + K (TS 2)	K Sparring	Break

Note: TS 1 = Training Session 1.

31

Stretching Program

The following stretching program can be used by everybody, and is a good general program for beginners as it deals with all important muscle groups. As your training progresses, you can adapt it to your individual requirements and your improved performance level. New exercises and variants of these introductory exercises can be found in the book *Fitness for Full-Contact Fighters* (Delp 2006).

Note that when you make adjustments to the program, you must make sure that your new program includes all muscle groups. Each group of muscles must always be stretched separately, before combining them into a more complex stretch. You may, for example, initially stretch the calf muscles prior to doing a complex stretch for the rear leg muscles. This way you avoid experiencing restrictions to the intensity of the exercise on account of tightness in the calf muscles.

Stretching method

The best-known form of stretching has two phases: light and progressive.

In the **light stretching phase,** you carefully select a position in which you only feel minor tension from the stretch. Maintain the position for a few seconds and consciously relax the muscle. Opinions differ on the exact execution of the stretch; I recommend counting up to 20 seconds, while remaining in this position. Once you have gained more experience, you will develop your own sense as to how much stretch time your body needs. The tension from the stretch should ease somewhat after a short period of time. Even if you do not feel the tension ease, you should feel comfortable enough in that position to be able to relax. Should this not be the case, you must relax the stretch a bit to reduce the tension.

In the **progressive stretching phase,** you will intensify the stretching position until a new tension can be felt, maintaining this new position for 20 seconds. This extended position should also be comfortable; otherwise, relax the stretch a bit to release some of the tension.

When you have finished both phases, carefully move out of the stretch position.

- Move your muscle slowly into a position, until you can feel light tension (first phase).
- Maintain the position for about 20 seconds.
- Extend the stretch until new tension can be felt (second phase).
- Maintain the position for about 20 seconds.
- Relax your muscles carefully as you move out of the stretch.

Guidelines

- Make sure that your starting position is stable—unsteadiness at a high stretching intensity may cause you exceed the optimum position and result in injury.
- Move slowly and cautiously, in order to find the correct stretch position. Abrupt movements may lead to serious injuries. Subsequently, use the same caution when moving out of the stretching position.
- Your performance level decides the stretching position. Do not attempt the same intensity as your partner in training or the individuals shown in the book. For guidance, use your own sense to guide how deep you go into a stretch, as all people have different physical preconditions. You will also discover that the tension in your muscles will be somewhat different from day to day.
- You must never attempt to reach a stretching position by force. If you feel pain, you must promptly ease the stretch position, as the muscle will continue to harden, not relax. Your agility will improve only if you slowly accustom the relaxed muscle to the new stretch position in regular exercises.
- Once you have found the correct position, concentrate on the muscle to be stretched. Relax the muscle and the entire muscular system.

- Breathe slowly and at regular intervals during stretching, and observe the relaxation in your muscle. Extensions to the stretching position are carried out while exhaling.
- Regular stretching is a prerequisite for long-term improvement and maintenance of your agility. Perform at least two stretching sessions a week and avoid lengthy breaks in between these sessions. You are not required to keep a minimum of two days between stretching sessions because correct stretching regenerates rather than strains the body.

Stretching Program

S1: Stretching the neck muscles. Start out standing with your legs shoulder-width apart. Lean your head to the right and lower the left arm. Place the right hand on the head and push it down gently to intensify the stretch. Switch and carry out the exercise on the left side.

S2: Stretching the chest and biceps. Start out in a lunge position, with one foot slightly in front of the other, and your arms raised in a U-shape. Simultaneously push your chest forward and your arms back until you feel a slight tension. Don't sink into the lunge position too much—bend your knees only a little.

S3: Stretching the lateral chest and back muscles. Stretch the left arm up into the air and lean with the upper part of your body to the right. Be sure to stay in line with the upper body, and do not move sideways. Subsequently, carry out the exercise to the left side.

S1

S2

S3

S4: Stretching the shoulder and upper back muscles. Cross your arms across your chest so that your hands are moving in the direction of your shoulder blades. The upper arms remain in a horizontal position. Advanced students should try to touch their shoulder blades.

S5: Stretching the shoulders, chest, and triceps. The right lower arm is pointing down behind the head, which will leave the upper arm in a vertical position. Use the left hand to apply pressure to the right elbow to intensify the stretch. Then carry out the exercise to the other side.

S6: Stretching the calf muscles. Move into a lunge position, with the rear leg slightly bent. Slowly stretch the rear leg, pushing the heel in the direction of the floor until you feel a slight tension.

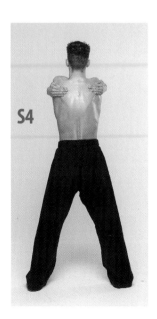
S4

S5

S6

S7: Stretching the hip flexors and the quadriceps (front thigh muscles). From an upright position take hold of the foot and move it as far as possible in the direction of the buttocks until you can feel a slight tension. In the process, you must consciously move your hip forward.

S8: Stretching the back and hamstrings (rear thigh muscles). Stand upright, with the feet close together; the legs should be stretched, but do not lock your knees. Slowly move your upper body toward your legs.

S9: Stretching the hamstrings, the hip flexors, and the quadriceps. From a lunge position, slowly push the hip and the front leg to the front until you experience a slight tension. Experts can do splits from this position.

S7

S8

S9

S10

S11

S12

S10: Stretching the inner and rear thigh and back muscles. From a standing position, spread your legs out until you feel a slight tension. Make sure that the hips do not shift back. Move your upper body first toward the right leg, then to the center, and then toward the left leg. Place your hands on the right leg when you move to the right; place your hands on the left leg when you move to the left. Maintain each position for a few seconds.

S11: Stretching the inner and rear thigh muscles, and back muscles. From a standing position, with widespread legs, place your hands on the floor behind you and take a seat on the ground, while maintaining the spread-leg position. Now stretch to the right side, to the center (leaning forward for a deeper stretch), and to the left side. Lean your upper body forward, as if you were being pulled, and simultaneously shift your hip to the front.

S12: Stretching the buttocks, outer thigh, and back muscles. Sit on the floor with both legs stretched out in front. Move your left leg as close as possible to the buttocks and cross it over the right leg. Push the knee with the right arm to the outside to intensify the stretch. In addition, you can bend the previously straight leg for extension of the stretching position.

32

Power Training Program

Power training will improve your performance in martial arts. Regular power training through a balanced program that exercises of all the body's muscle groups is recommended. Additional strength improves your power in punching, pushing, and kicking. In addition, strong muscles enable you to better withstand an opponent's blows. Lastly, in kickboxing some muscle groups are exerted more than others, which makes the athlete susceptible to injuries. Regular power training can prevent the development of such muscle imbalances.

The following exercises have been selected because they are particularly suited for kickboxers and help you strengthen all muscle groups in a balanced way. The exercises can be carried out with dumbbells at home.

Optional exercises can be found in the book *Fitness for Full-Contact Fighters* (Delp 2006).

Program Structure

Each session of your program should be divided into three phases: warm-up, main workout, and cool-down. Organize your fitness training accordingly.

Warm-up

Start the program with an exercise that warms up the body and prepares it for the strain of training. Choose an exercise that can be carried out at a steady pace for 5–10 minutes, like easy jogging, skipping rope, or an easy routine on a stationary bike. Do not lose your breath. Do not overexert yourself or perform any quick or jolting moves. This phase is meant to get your body adjusted to the training, not to achieve maximum performance.

Once you have warmed up your body, start with the stretching exercises. It is best to intensively stretch all the muscle groups, but for a short training session, it will also suffice to stretch those muscle groups that will be exercised in the main section. Without prior stretching, there will be a risk of injury, and the body will not be properly prepared for the exercise and thus will not be able to deliver maximum performance. Plan a minimum of five minutes for the preparatory stretching of individual muscle groups. However, the time can be extended, particularly if you wish to improve your flexibility.

Power Training

Perform the exercises described below in accordance with their instructions. Repeat the execution for as often as is required by the training method you use. You must select a weight that permits technically correct repetitions—without wrong positioning or incorrect compensatory movements. Although an exercise is described for one side only, it should be done on both sides, as both sides of the body must always be strengthened together.

Cool-down

After a training session, you should cool down to relax the muscles. This also helps the body to regenerate quickly. Move at an easy pace for about five minutes, without effort. Particularly suitable are walking, slow jogging, and cycling at low intensity.

At the end of your fitness training, stretch out the activated muscles once more. Do not attempt any extreme stretching positions, as the muscles are tired and tend to cramp. Stretching at the end of training serves to loosen the body and prevent shrinking of the muscles.

Training Methods

Martial arts athletes concentrate their training either on the stamina power method or the muscle development method. The primary aims of stamina power training are a slender body and good stamina, whereas the muscle development method is aimed at the development of a muscular body and the strengthening of muscle power. Untrained athletes must initially improve their stamina power before they start to develop their muscle power.

Stamina Power Method	
Users:	Beginners, advanced, and competitive athletes
Repetitions:	15–30
Speed:	Slow to swift
Intensity per set (subjective):	Medium to hard
Break between two sets:	1–2 minutes
Training targets:	Stamina improvement, reduction of body fat

Muscle Development Method

Users:	Beginners, advanced, and competitive athletes
Repetitions:	8–12
Speed:	Slow
Intensity per set (subjective):	Hard to very hard
Break between two sets:	2–3 minutes
Training targets:	Muscle development, increase in maximum power

Guidelines

Make sure your starting position is stable, so that you can fully concentrate on the execution of your exercise. Tense your abdominal muscles to stabilize the upper body, and keep your back straight. Exercises in a standing position will also activate the buttocks muscles.

Prior to exercising with dumbbells always check their fastenings, particularly if you plan to lift them above your head.

Perform each exercise with regular, rather slow movements and pay attention to a technically correct execution. The aim of power training is the effective training of the muscles, not the lifting of maximum weight. Concentrate on the target muscles and consciously experience how they work during training. The muscles being trained must be kept active during the complete exercise.

Regularly monitor the starting position and the exercise execution by practicing in front of a mirror. Make sure that the shoulders remain at the same level. Bending the wrists during an exercise increases the risk of tendonitis.

Maintain regular breathing during exercises that use light weights and low intensity, and during those carried out slowly or statically. If you interrupt the rhythm of your breath, your body will receive insufficient oxygen, which poses a considerable health risk. If you carry out exercises with heavy weights, high intensity, and high speed, inhale prior to each move, exhale during the exertion, and inhale again when you return to the starting position. Maintain this rhythm during all repetitions. If the end position is maintained for a few seconds for intensification, continue to breathe regularly.

You may strain and exhaust yourself during the exercises—stamina power training requires many repetitions, and muscle development training requires heavy weights. However, if you experience pain, the exercise must be stopped immediately. If the pain decreases during the rest break, consider the reason for the pain—for example, a wrong body stance—and try again. If the same pain reappears, stop the exercise and continue with the next one in your training plan. If the pain doesn't disappear during the rest break, stop your training and consult a physician.

Always perform your exercises for the left and right side of your body with the same intensity, for balanced training of your body. All important muscle groups must be included in the training program.

You can change the shape of your body only by regular exercise. Beginners should train at least twice per week, advanced athletes more often. If you pause for longer periods, your muscle strength and size will slowly decrease. If you are sick, however, you shouldn't train, as training may jeopardize the healing process.

Beginners should carry out the exercises with little strain. It is better to choose weights/intensities that are too low rather than too high. Muscles get used to new demands quicker than do tendons and ligaments, which is why the body must be accustomed slowly to an intensification of exercise. Increase the number of repetitions and sets before increasing the weights/intensities. If the demands increase too rapidly, the body will be in danger of being hurt.

Power Program: Whole Body

2–3 sets	K1–K7: 8–12 repetitions or 15–20 repetitions in one set. (depending on the training goal)
	K8: maintain 30–60 seconds in one set

K1: Push-up

Strengthening of the chest, shoulders, and triceps.

Support your weight with your hands and toes and lower yourself to the floor. Your hands should be shoulder-width apart with the fingers pointing forward. Tighten the abdominal muscles and the muscles of the buttocks for stabilization of the back. Look down, but keep your head stable, and don't let it droop.

Bend your arms until the upper body nearly touches the floor, but do not rest on the ground. Then straighten the arms and return to your starting position. Be sure to keep your back straight during the exercise.

Changing your hand position will have an effect on different parts of the chest muscle. Well-trained athletes can place their toes on an object, thereby intensifying the exercise.

K2: One-Arm Dumbbell Row

Strengthening of the upper back, biceps, neck, and rear shoulder muscles.

Step into a lunge and support your weight by placing one hand on the front thigh. The other arm holds the dumbbell (palm facing the body), and starts off straight. The back is straight, and the abdominal muscles and the muscles of the buttocks are tight.

Pull the elbow back and up as far as possible to the rear, keeping the upper arm close to the body. Then slowly lower the arm, but do not completely straighten it. Avoid raising the shoulder throughout the exercise, and pay attention to keeping your upper body straight.

For better support, you can place the front hand on a chair or other object.

K3: Overhead Press

Strengthening of the shoulder muscles (particularly the lateral part), the neck, and the triceps.

Sit erect on a chair, bench, or other stable object. Your arms are bent so that they form right angles; the elbows point to the outside, so that your head is between the dumbbells. Hold the dumbbells with the thumbs pointing toward each other. Tighten the abdominal muscles.

Raise both dumbbells at the same time, without changing your hand position. Extend the arms all the way up. Keep your back straight. Return your arms slowly to the starting position. Avoid moving your head forward or allowing the dumbbells to move to the front or rear.

K4: Squat

Strengthening of the thigh, buttocks, calf, and lower back muscles.

Stand upright with the knees slightly bent. Spread the feet a bit more than shoulder-width apart, and point the toes slightly outward. Hold dumbbells in your hands, with your palms facing you. Tighten the abdominal muscles and keep the back straight.

Bend the knees as low as possible, and, in the process, press your buttocks backward. Keep your back straight and keep the knees above the feet, not forward or to the side. Straighten your legs, and lift your heels at the end of the move.

K5: Hip Lift

Strengthening of the thigh muscles (particularly the rear thigh), buttocks, and lower back muscles.

Lie on your back. Draw your legs toward you by bending the knees, and rest the heels on the floor. The knee joints form an angle of about ninety degrees. Tighten the abdominal muscles and press the heels toward the ground.

To start the exercise, push the heels hard against the ground and raise the hips so that the thighs and the back are in a straight line. Now lower and raise the hips several times without rest. Be sure to breathe evenly and keep the abdominal muscles tight.

Advanced athletes can perform this exercise with one leg raised, as pictured.

K6: Crunch

Strengthening of the abdominal muscles.

Lie on your back, with your legs bent; you can rest your heels on the ground or up on an object, as pictured. Apply some pressure with your heels to keep from making your back hollow during the exercise.

Slowly raise your upper body, and at the same time, pull the chin slightly toward the chest. The entire move is generated by the abdominal muscles—do not use a swinging motion. Hold the end position for about three seconds while you tighten the abdominal muscles at maximum strength and maintain regular breathing. Then slowly lower the upper body, but do not rest it on the floor, so that the muscles remain tight.

K7: Lateral Plank

Strengthening of the abdominal, outer thigh, and shoulder muscles.

You are in a side position with your forearm resting on the floor below the shoulder. The hip and the lower leg rest on the floor. Build up tension between the lower arm and the foot.

Raise the hips and thigh, so that only the outer side of the foot touches the floor. Maintain the position for a few seconds before you lower the hips. Do not lower the hips all the way down to the floor as

you repeat the exercise. Pay attention to regular breathing, and avoid making compensatory twisting movements with the upper body.

You can intensify the exercise by raising the upper leg and extending your upper arm above the head.

K8: Raising the Body from a Prone Position

Strengthening the lower back, neck, rear shoulder, and rear thigh muscles.

Lie on the floor in a prone position, with your arms extended over your head. Both arms and your forehead should rest on the floor. Tighten the abdominal muscles and the muscles of the buttocks, and raise the head, arms, and legs simultaneously. The arms are raised higher than the head; the forehead remains parallel to the floor. This end position is maintained for 30–60 seconds. Be sure to keep your breathing even and regular, and abdominal muscles tight.

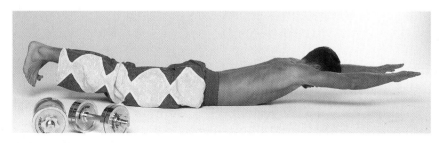

Part IX
Competition

Contest Guidelines

33

To succeed in a kickboxing contest you must observe the following rules in respect to fight preparation and fight conduct.

Preparation

High competitive aims can only be achieved through proper preparation. You must assume that you will meet an opponent whose technical and physical performance is as high as yours, if not higher. Proper preparation can provide you with the opportunity to gain an advantage, which will be decisive for the victory.

In the course of prepping for a fight, you must eliminate all stress factors that could distract you from your training in the following weeks. Speak to your partner, family, and friends and inform them of your plan, so that they are aware of and sensitive to the intensive process you'll be going through.

Your training schedule must be challenging and your weight must be strictly controlled. Only athletes who are hard on themselves will develop the optimum performance levels and the correct mental approach for the contest. The lifestyle of a fighter must be tailored to the athletic competition (i.e., you might need more sleep than usual, and therefore, you should maintain a regular sleep schedule). Use regenerative measures, such as sauna and massage to help speed up recovery time, thereby preventing excessive physical strain.

Intensive preparation is also important for self-confidence—knowing you're performing at an optimum level will increase your self-assurance in a match.

Weighing In

If on the day of the fight, you exceed the weight limit, you can still quickly lose two to three pounds by sweating. The maximum is three pounds, as shedding that much water weight before a fight will already reduce your performance, and shedding any more is dangerous. Kickboxers frequently prefer skipping rope or jogging for sweating. The athlete wears warm clothes to increase the body temperature and to generate more sweat. Skipping should be at an even pace, but not at a high pulse rate, to save energy for the fight. Subsequently, the skin is firmly rubbed with towels, which can reduce the weight a little further.

Drink plenty of fluids—water and fitness drinks—after weighing in, however, do so slowly. Eat easily digestible food and chew slowly. Fitness bars and bananas are recommended. Do not eat too much, avoid fatty or spicy foods, and avoid foods that you are not accustomed to, as these may cause stomach cramps. If you have sufficient time prior to the contest, you can have another easily digestible portion about one hour after the first small meal.

Conduct Prior to the Fight

Concentrate on the contest and collect your thoughts. Visualize your long and ascetic training and keep in mind that you can now demonstrate why you went through the grueling process. You must completely concentrate on the fight, and you must not be concerned about anything else. Your training staff must protect you from any external influence that could take your mind off the fight. It is therefore important to be surrounded by individuals you can trust.

Start warming up at an early stage. After the usual warm-up exercises and stretching it is recommended to carry out light shadowboxing and to go over the fight tactics with your trainer. Also, do a warm-up on pads to gain a feeling for distance. You should avoid intensive training on the pads with powerful techniques, thus not wasting any energy before the fight. You must, though, clearly increase your pulse rate a number of times, so that you are warmed up enough to call on your full performance from the start of round one—this way an opponent rushing toward you at the sound of the bell won't catch you by surprise. You can increase your pulse rate by shadowboxing, skipping rope, and through swift, but not powerful work on the pads.

Fight Conduct

Enter the ring or the fight area with self-assurance. Breathe evenly and stay relaxed. Pay particular attention to your neck muscles, keeping them consciously relaxed, as some athletes get very tense prior to a contest and apply extreme tension to their neck muscles. Nervousness prior to the contest differs from athlete to athlete and improves throughout the athlete's career. If you enter the ring hyped-up and nervous, you lose valuable energy for the fight. Visualize your strong points.

Know that you are now prepared to fight. Take pride in your intensive training and look forward to showing off your hard-won skills.

Carry out some relaxed moves in the ring to get a feeling for the ring and the floor. Fall back lightly into the ropes to get a feeling for the tension. Think of your fight tactics; you must be prepared for your opponent to rush you as soon as the fight starts.

Welcome the opponent prior to the fight and show respect for his athletic performance. Remember that he has also endured a long and ascetic preparation. Your objective is, however, to win, so you are now permitted to do whatever you need to do to win the fight as long as it conforms to the rules. Give the impression that you are convinced of your victory. In contact kickboxing, you can also intimidate your opponent by gestures, e.g. by staring aggressively into his eyes. Some means of provocation are, however, not acceptable, including abuse, spitting, and the conscious use of illegal techniques (e.g. attacks to the genitals). If an athlete does this repeatedly, he will be disqualified.

Concentrate on the contest and do not let your rhythm be disturbed by calls from the audience. Always stay in control, keep your cool, and resist any temptation for rash action or overly hasty counterattacks. If you fight without control, you'll be in danger of being hit by an effective counter technique, which may cause you to lose the fight early on. Avoid being drawn into wild exchanges of punches and kicks, and always maintain control of the respective fight situation.

Keep moving and use the entire area of the ring. Avoid being driven into a corner—always move away to the side if you feel yourself backing up into the ropes. If you remain in a fixed position, the opponent will find it easy to figure you out.

Always maintain a strong fight stance, and move with confidence—you want to show your opponent that you are still fit and able to fight. Mislead the opponent, feint, and keep him on the move. Never show any weakness or pain. If the opponent realizes that you have been affected by a technique and that you have a weak point, he will concentrate on this part of the body. Even when you are hit by an effective blow, you must create the impression to the audience and the referees that the opponent's technique was harmless. This can demoralize an opponent in a hard fight and can be the decisive edge in the final count.

After the fight you respectfully bid goodbye to the opponent. He did his best, and this must be respected.

After the fight, congratulate your opponent. Even after a hard fight, it is important to pay respects to the opponent's performance.

Break between Rounds

Prior to the fight it is important for you and your trainer to agree upon the exact conduct during breaks. If the coach sees that you are moving slowly after the bell, he must promptly come toward you and walk with you to your corner. People should not get the impression that you are groggy, even though you might be.

You must rest and relax during the break, concentrate, and take deep breaths in preparation for the next round. The coach can massage your neck, which is of particular importance if you are tense and nervous.

The coach must give you clear and precise directions for the next round. Pay no attention to other people shouting irrelevant information from outside the ring. It is also of no help to you, if the coach accompanies his explanations with nervous gestures. You must be able to rely on only one person to give you precise directions on your fight conduct. Such directions can relate to your mistakes, the opponent's weak points, and recommendations on counter techniques. The coach may demand that you repeat the tactics for the fight in detail, so that they are better engrained in your memory.

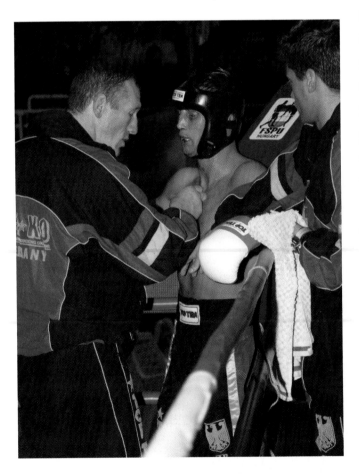

Ferdinand Mack coaches a fighter.

Between Tournament Bouts

Always keep warm by shadowboxing and stretching between matches. Prior to each contest in the tournament, particularly after a lengthy break, it is important that you increase your pulse rate by easy punches and kicks to the pads or by skipping rope. You must also prepare for the tactics of each fight with easy shadowboxing.

Drink plenty of fluids between the contests, especially water, mineral water, and fitness drinks. Bananas and fitness bars are recommended as food. Do not eat too much and avoid spicy or fatty foods. You must also stay away from foods that you are not accustomed to, as these may lead to stomach cramps.

Post-Fight Recovery

After a fight, give your body a rest from training. This will help your body regenerate, and will help you regain a clear head and accumulate new energy. The body requires some time to recover after several weeks of fight preparation, before you can start with the next training program. This procedure is important, in order to be able to achieve progressive performance improvements and, eventually, maximum performance. The regeneration phase must be extended in

accordance with the intensity of the preparatory phase and the fight effort. You should resume soft sport activities, though, no later than one week after the fight. This could include, for example, easy jogging at a low heart rate, to ensure that your physical performance does not deteriorate and your weight does not increase significantly. A complete rest of more than one week will have a negative effect on your performance level.

Interview with Martin Albers,
World, European, and German Champion

How many years did you compete? How did you overcome difficulties in motivation?

I initially competed in All-Style Karate in 1991. The fight style was very close to Semi-Contact Kickboxing. Our training group at the time participated regularly in tournaments. When I changed to training with Peter Zaar in Cologne in 1996, my training developed more and more in the direction of competitive sport. The results were systematic training plans and a long-term tournament calendar. From 1997 to 2002 I was a member of the national squad and competed in more than one hundred contests.

You certainly experience peaks and troughs during that time. Both my trainer and my training partners continued to motivate me to go on. In addition, the regular rhythm of training and the success always were incentives to compete in more tournaments. It was the change in my business career and the inherent obligations that put a stop to my competitive efforts.

How often did you train per week? How did you organize the last week of training before a contest?

Depending on the annual plan and the tournament dates, I achieved different performance levels in training. Throughout the general and special preparatory phases, I trained four to five times a week. As these weeks did not include any competition I did not train at maximum load, but I did extend the training sessions. The training increased in mid-February and mid-August, due to upcoming tournaments on the annual plan. In the immediate preparation for a contest, the most intensive training phase of the year, I trained up to twenty sessions per week. These alternated between a regenerative long-distance run in the morning and highly demanding dual sessions with plenty of sparring in the evening.

The last week of training was always planned at low load. The body must have the opportunity for a complete rest and must recharge the batteries. Only a fully fit and regenerated body can achieve the desired performance in a tournament. In addition, it is possible to carry out resilience exercises until a short time before the contest. This, however, should not be too much of a strain on the cardiovascular system.

How did you eat? Did you take supplements?

I always ensured that my body received all the vital energy carriers, vitamins, and minerals. I did not adhere to a detailed nutritional plan. It's important not to eat any heavy meals before training or before bedtime. Apart from plenty of fruits and vegetables, the body must be given plenty of fluids. In times of intensive training, I added meals with plenty of carbohydrates. In the normal preparatory phase, in which I did additional power training, I also took protein supplements.

In which weight division did you compete? Did you ever have difficulties making weight? How did you reduce your weight in the last week before a fight?

In the last ten years, I did not have a problem to maintain my weight between 180 and 187 lb. I never had any problems to achieve my competitive weight. I'm aware that I am very lucky in this respect.

In the last week of training before a fight, I concentrate on eating a very low-fat diet. Many carbohydrates, usually noodles, were on my menu. I frequently observed many hard-working competitors trying to shed six to nine pounds before tournaments. Although this usually worked, the athletes often felt tired in their contests and were unable to perform at normal levels.

How often did you warm up prior to a contest? How did you prepare for and concentrate on a fight?

In my studies at Cologne University, I learned a lot about competitive psychology. I was able to use this knowledge in many ways. As I frequently knew the fight style of my opponents beforehand, I could analyze the contests in my head before the actual fight. I was already able to visualize previously trained strategies.

As the starting time of a tournament contest can never be exactly predicted, I began my warm-up early and kept myself warm throughout the day. Short stretching exercises were added. Once the next fight drew closer, I increased my pulse rate by intensive pre-loads. You should never enter the ring cold.

During professional fights, I would start my warm-up program approximately one hour before the call. This way, I had sufficient time to prepare my body and head for the contest.

What did you eat and drink before and between tournament contests?

Prior to and throughout the tournaments I ate little, but drank lots. The body should not be upset with food that's difficult to digest. Light snacks, such as fruits, muesli bars, and also chocolate, are quick and effective energy suppliers. On the day of competition I drank four to five liters of water or sports drinks.

How do you describe your fight style?

My trainer, Peter Zaar, aims to develop universal kickboxers. With me, he did not succeed completely. A universal kickboxer is very variable and able to impose his fight style on any other type of fighter. I see myself rather as a kickboxer who tries to fight at high pace. I also always tried to keep my opponents busy with different combinations of foot and fist techniques from long distance.

How did you approach a close-distance fighter (boxer)?

In the case of a strong boxer, I tried to avoid close distance as much as possible. The typical close-distance fighter in my weight division was usually smaller and stronger than I. He was, thus, able to make better use of fist techniques at close distance. I kept the opponent at bay with straight kicks of the front leg, such as front kicks and side kicks. To the foot techniques I added fist combinations. These were normally three swift straight punches. The back kick also proved to be a good weapon against an onrushing boxer.

How did you approach a distance fighter (kicker)?

This type of fighter represented more of my fight style. I used to have particular problems with good tae kwon do athletes. In these cases, I tried to bridge the distance at an earlier stage and start with fist combinations. A cautious approach is required, as distance fighters aim their kicks to keep their opponents at some distance.

How do you fight a quick acting and tricky opponent?

The aim is to impose your fight style on the opponent. I have always tried to dictate the distance and the time of attack in a fight. Quick opponents frequently fight at high pace. I must stop this pace, as quick technically versed fighters usually are in very good physical condition. In this case, long foot techniques are effective weapons, keeping the opponent away. Tricky opponents like to provoke. With feints, you generate the opponent's defensive or attacking reactions.

How do you fight a southpaw?

Against southpaws, I always tried to move from right to left. Moving to the right entails the risk of running into his strong left punch. Moving to the left offers better control of his jab and I can start with foot and fist combinations of my own. For me, fighting from a conventional stance, it is important never to start or conclude an attack against a southpaw with the rear leg. In all fights, I always protected my attacks with the front hand or the front leg. In the case of a southpaw, this rule is of even greater importance.

Do you have special tips to help a kickboxer succeed in competition?

As a matter of principle, all kickboxers should only register for a contest once they are prepared to face the high mental strain. Good preparation is required for success. The decision for a fight should primarily be made by the athlete and not by the people around him or her. On the day of the contest, the athlete should not be bothered too much by others. This only leads to more stress, which takes an extreme toll on energy. On the other hand, a contest must not be approached too relaxed, as the fight requires a maximum of concentration and alertness. Such concentration and alertness is achieved by a "sound" measure of nervousness and stage fright.

The success in competition should not be measured in terms of placement. Success in competition means that the training results can be properly and successfully converted into practice under new conditions.

Are you planning an active future as trainer?

For the time being, I try to attend Peter Zaar's training regularly as a student. I will continue to train in the coming years under competitive conditions. I am unable to foresee for how long this will be possible. I do not rule out a return to competitive contests. This must, though, be compatible with my business life. As an entrepreneur, this is not really easy. I could certainly imagine training my own students in kickboxing sometime in the future. I've completed my trainer education courses in kickboxing, so I now have the necessary prerequisites.

34

Fight Tactics

The tactics of a kickboxer are of vital significance to achieving high competitive aims. Whether or not the kickboxer succeeds in imposing his fight style on the match and, thereby, controlling the action, is of decisive importance to the outcome of a contest.

Typical Mistakes

Certain mistakes arise in contests time and again and must definitely be avoided.

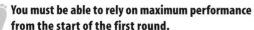 **You must be able to rely on maximum performance from the start of the first round.**

Slow Start

You must be focused and ready to deliver your techniques from the moment the bell rings. If you start the first round slowly and passively, you will frequently be unable to compensate for the lost points in the following rounds. This applies particularly to amateur kickboxing, in which contests are scheduled for few rounds only. A loss of points from the first round can also mean that the original fight tactics must be abandoned to score points through aggressive action. Such an approach is, however, rarely successful and instead entails the great risk that you move into an opponent's hard technique, which could be the early end of the fight for you.

Overly Hasty Start

If you rush toward your opponent in the first round and attack with wild punches—aiming to break his will and self-assurance or even to succeed in a premature end of the fight—you will waste much power and energy. Success in such an exchange of blows is determined by physical preconditions and not by the tactics of kickboxing. You do not learn anything about the fight conduct and the mistakes of the opponent, which is vital for the rest of the contest. For the opponent, it is usually relatively easy to defend the onrush and, once your stamina is affected on account of the intensive attack, he can counter effectively. It is a rule that fighters who start the first round with undue haste experience considerable physical difficulties in the subsequent rounds.

Passive and One-Sided Fight Style

Do not restrict your fight style to passive defense measures. If you react primarily with defensive techniques and without subsequent counters, the opponent can continue his attack without interruption. You should always follow up your defensive techniques with attacking techniques of your own.

Maintain your concentration, and do not get nervous and adopt the opponent's fight style. Stay versatile and do not just use a limited number of techniques, as this makes it easy for the opponent to figure you out. Often athletes concentrate on boxing techniques and use only few kicking techniques. This approach leaves you unable to prepare for effective techniques and combinations—you'll have to wait until the opponent offers you the opportunity for the application of a technique.

Fight Styles

The following fight styles can frequently be seen in the ring and you must learn their defense by heart. Bear in mind that the opponent can change his fight tactics in the course of the contest.

Back kicks are a suitable defense against an on-rushing opponent.

Fighters with Special Techniques

These fighters have mastered a particular offensive technique, one that they employ often. This can be a punching technique, such as a rear straight punch, or a kicking technique, such as a front hook kick. The application of this attacking technique is frequently a great danger for their opponent.

Try to stop the use of this technique. If the opponent, for example, is known for a powerful rear straight punch, you can repeatedly deliver techniques to the opponent's punching arm (e.g. roundhouse kicks with the rear leg). Several kicks to the upper arm can also foil the opponent's effective use of his special technique. You must also study the opponent and figure out in which fight situations he usually delivers his special technique. If you are successful, you can feint, causing him to carry out his special technique. Since you are now expecting the technique, you will be able to avoid the blow and counter with an effective technique of your own.

Distance Fighters

Rather tall fighters with particular kicking skills frequently attempt to conduct the contest from a distance. You must bridge the distance to the opponent to be able to deliver effective attacks from a medium or close range. If possible, push the opponent into the corner of the ring and work with hooks to the body and head. Use feints and quick combinations to set up the chance to move forward. If you are successful with a feint or if you land a combination, then you can move forward. Keep your upper body in motion, so that you do not offer a fixed target. If you have the opportunity for a forward move, for example after deflection of a technique to the side, you must move in a flash with your guard raised. However, if this is carried out too quickly and the opponent reads your intention, he will launch an effective counter attack.

Some distance fighters specialize in counter techniques. These fighters require versatile reactions. The opponent tries to figure you out, enabling him to read your techniques at an early stage and to deliver effective counters. You must, therefore, work with many evasive moves and feints, so that he leaves his position and you can perform different combinations.

Close-Distance Fighters

Powerful fighters with strong boxing skills frequently look for ways to keep the fight distance close, allowing them to deliver effective punching techniques. You must try to keep the opponent at a distance, so that he cannot use his skills. Use jabs, front kicks, and side kicks of the front leg. These techniques will keep him away, interrupting his techniques, and enabling you to set up your combinations. Avoid exchanging punches with these fighters. If the opponent rushes forward, do not let yourself be pushed back into the corner—step away to the side. You should also do feints, tempting him to rush forward, so that you can counter with an effective technique.

Swift and Tricky Fighters

These athletes move with quick steps toward and away from the opponent. They deliver quick combinations and use many feints and evasive moves. Do not be misled and attempt to adopt the opponent's fight pace; instead, try to maintain your own fight style. Take position in the center of the ring, hold this position, and study the opponent's fight conduct. In the process, you also try to maintain the best suitable distance by keeping him busy. You must, however, not follow him hastily, but should move and turn along with him from the center of the ring.

Deliver strong punches and kicks to restrict his movements. If you succeed with a blow and he loses his sense of coordination somewhat, you must quickly follow up with powerful punching techniques. You then try to push him into the corner of the ring, to fix him in the corner and continue your attacks.

Fighter in a Different Stance

In the case of a hard-hitting fighter, who uses a different stance than you, you must make sure you do not move to the side of the opponent's rear punching arm. You can keep the opponent away with front kicks and jabs. You should also repeatedly deliver combinations that include a front hook, in the process of which you move to the outside, away from the punching arm. In a conventional stance against a southpaw, you should move left to the outside; a southpaw against a fighter with a conventional stance should move right to the outside.

If the opponent uses a large number of front jabs and front-leg front kicks, reduce the target area as much as possible. Study his fight conduct in detail and use counter techniques, which stop the success of the opponent's jabs and front kicks. The opponent will turn to more and more techniques from the rear part of his body. These techniques are easier to identify and defend against.

35

Making Weight

To become eligible for a kickboxing competition you and your trainer must determine which weight division you will fight in, and then concentrate your training on maintaining this weight. Many factors must be considered in the determination of the best-suited weight division, such as a fighter's current weight, percentage of body fat, fight style, and the level of competition.

The percentage of body fat should be as low as possible, eight to ten percent for professional male kickboxing athletes, and slightly higher for female athletes. Body-fat percentage can also be somewhat higher in amateurs, who do not have to face the same competitive demands. A high degree of fat means that the athlete is not fully trained; athletes must compete in a higher weight division, in which the opponents will likely be bigger and stronger. In this situation, athletes can survive only if they are technically superior.

If the kickboxer's percentage of body fat is 15 percent, it can be reduced by 6 percent down to 9 percent through intensive training and proper nutrition. This means that a fighter weighing 170 pounds can reduce his body fat by 10.2 pounds without losing performance capabilities. Further slimming can be achieved only by a reduction in muscle mass, which leads to less strength and a deterioration in performance. Experience shows that it gets progressively more difficult to lose body fat the closer you come to the optimal area. For example, it is easier to achieve a reduction from 15 to 13 percent than from 12 to 10 percent.

If you want to keep track of your body's development, you can check your weight, your percentage of body fat, and your body's dimensions at regular intervals. Measure the size of the upper arms, chest, waist, hips, thighs, and calves, as these parts show the clearest changes. The aim is to achieve a narrow waist, while the other parts increase in size. Accordingly, examine the waist at its most narrow point and all other parts at their largest point. Record the results on a checklist.

The primary aim of competitive athletes who are above their weight limit despite a relatively low percentage of fat is to reduce the size of the waist and to maintain or slightly reduce the size of the other body parts. Record the results in your training journal. This procedure is also recommended if you do not wish to participate in competition, but only want to concentrate on the fitness benefits of kickboxing.

Nutritional Objective: Maintaining the Fighting Weight

If it is your objective to simultaneously improve your kickboxing performance while maintaining your fighting weight, you must be sure that your caloric intake corresponds more or less to your calorie out-

put. This applies equally to kickboxing, stamina training, and power training. Eat healthy foods, such as lean meat, fish, whole-grain products, fruits, fresh vegetables, and vital fats.

Do not exercise on an empty stomach. Consume sufficient carbohydrates and protein prior to training. It is best to eat your biggest meal approximately three hours prior to training and to eat a carbohydrate-rich snack, such as a banana, about an hour before you start. You will then be able to call on your optimum performance during training. It is also worthwhile to eat a fitness bar during a lengthy, very intensive training session. Drinking lots of fluids during training is a must. After the training session, concentrate on foods rich in carbohydrates and protein, so that the body receives the nutrients required for regeneration.

Food Guidelines

- Choose nutrients geared toward optimal caloric output.

- Consume high-grade carbohydrates.

  Whole-grain products are best.

- Consume moderate proportions of proteins.

  Low-fat meats (lean turkey), fish, and legumes (peas and beans) are best.

- Consume only moderate amounts of fat.

  High-quality fats with simple unsaturated fatty acids and omega-3 fatty acids are best.

- Drink plenty of fluids.

  Water, apple juice diluted with water, and energy drinks are best during training.

- You may use supplements to promote quicker regeneration, but this is not essential.

Nutritional Objective: Losing Weight

If you want to reduce body fat to be able to compete in a lower weight division, you must add many stamina- and power-training sessions to your training. The caloric intake must be below your output. To ensure that you do not also reduce muscle volume, you must increase the proportion of protein with a corresponding reduction in carbohydrates. Follow a low-fat diet, but do not neglect the valuable fats. It is also essential to drink plenty of fluids.

Two to three hours before training, eat foods rich in protein (for example, a protein shake), and one to two hours before training, eat foods rich in carbohydrates (for example, a banana). This is of particular importance prior to power training; otherwise, you will feel drained. After the training session, have a meal rich in both carbohydrates and protein. However, don't consume too many carbohydrates or the calorie-burning effect of training will be offset. Do not abstain from carbohydrates completely, as this would have a negative effect on the protein in the muscles.

Food Guidelines

- Set your caloric intake lower than your caloric output.
- Consume a low proportion of carbohydrates.
  Choose products with a low glycemic index, and choose whole-grain products as often as possible.
- Consume a high proportion of protein.
  Lean turkey, low-fat cheese and cottage cheese, whey, legumes, and fish are best.
- Eat a low proportion of fat.
  High-quality fats containing simple unsaturated fatty acids are best.
- Drink a lot of fluids, especially water.
- Consuming amino-acid supplements helps to maintain muscle mass, but this is not essential.

Nutritional Objective: Gaining Weight

If you want to significantly increase muscle mass to be able to enter a higher weight division, you will need to add a rigorous muscle build-up training to the kickboxing training. To avoid excessive training you must reduce the kickboxing-specific training sessions. You must also increase your caloric intake, particularly the amount of protein you ingest. So that you do not increase the proportion of body fat along the way, you have to adhere to a low-fat diet. This will not lead to a fat deficiency, as the increase in food will also increase the amount of fat.

Two to three hours before power training, consume a meal rich in protein (for example, a protein shake with oatmeal), and one to two hours before training, eat a carbohydrate-rich snack (for example, a fitness bar). During training, you must drink plenty of fluids. Eating a protein bar halfway through is also recommended, so that the protein is available to the body immediately after training. After the training session, start to recharge the empty carbohydrate battery, and consume more protein at the same time. You should also eat plenty of protein-rich foods on days without power training, so that the body receives sufficient protein for muscle development.

Food Guidelines

- Increase your caloric intake in the build-up phase.
- Somewhat increase the supply of carbohydrates.
  Noodles, rice, and fitness bars are best.
- High protein is required.
  Protein (whey) shakes, protein bars, fish, lean meat, low-fat cottage cheese, and legumes are best.
- Consume a low proportion of fat.
- Drink a lot of fluids, especially water.
- Amino-acid and creatine supplements can be taken for muscle build-up, but these are not essential.

36

Fight Preparation

High athletic objectives demand a detailed training program. There is, however, no program applicable to all kickboxers. You must develop a program tailored to your particularities and requirements.

The following is a sample training program that will get a fighter reasonably prepared for contests. Adapt the plan to meet your requirements.

Eight-Week Training Program for Competition

This program shows how advanced kickboxers may organize an eight-week training cycle in preparation for a fight. This plan should only serve as a suggestion, as individual particularities, such as the necessary reduction of weight for a certain weight division, cannot be taken into account.

Interval runs are runs done over a pre-determined period and at different speeds. They alternate quick runs over a short distance (sprints) with easy jogging until the pulse rate has gone down. This procedure is repeated a number of times. The last ten minutes of the run are dedicated to slow jogging.

A whole-body program of 8–10 exercises is recommended for **power training**. In the last weeks of training prior to the contest the intensity of the power program should be reduced. Concentrate on basic exercises, which activate a large number of muscle groups. (Also recommended are exercises K1–K4, K6, and K8 detailed in Chapter 32.)

Maintain proper **nutrition** in accordance with your requirements to obtain optimum training results and minimize the risk of injury and infection. Be sure to eat enough protein to fuel all of your training and regenerative needs.

Sleep more than usual to aid the body's **regeneration**. Regenerative measures, such as massages and sauna sessions at least once a week, are also recommended.

Week 1	Day 1	Kickboxing
	Day 2	Jogging at medium intensity for 40–60 minutes
	Day 3	Power training (whole-body program)
	Day 4	Kickboxing
	Day 5	Jogging at low intensity for 40–60 minutes
	Day 6	Kickboxing (emphasis on sparring)
	Day 7	Rest
Week 2	Day 1	Kickboxing
	Day 2	Interval runs for 40–60 minutes
	Day 3	Power training (whole-body program)
	Day 4	Kickboxing
	Day 5	Jogging at low intensity for 40–60 minutes
	Day 6	Kickboxing (emphasis on sparring)
	Day 7	Rest
Week 3	Day 1	Kickboxing
	Day 2	Interval runs for 40–60 minutes
	Day 3	Power training (whole-body program)
	Day 4	Kickboxing
	Day 5	Jogging at medium intensity for 40–60 minutes
	Day 6	Kickboxing (emphasis on sparring)
	Day 7	Rest
Week 4	Day 1	Kickboxing
	Day 2	Interval runs (with short sprints) for 40–60 minutes
	Day 3	Kickboxing
	Day 4	Power training (whole-body program)
	Day 5	Kickboxing (emphasis on sparring)
	Day 6	Swimming or bicycling
	Day 7	Rest

After the contest, you should take a few days off for **recuperation**. After one week of rest, you should resume light training, such as jogging at low intensity. You now determine a new training cycle.

Week 5	Day 1	Kickboxing (emphasis on competitive tactics)
	Day 2	Power training (basic exercises)
	Day 3	Kickboxing (emphasis on sparring)
	Day 4	Kickboxing (emphasis on competitive tactics)
	Day 5	Interval runs (with short sprints) for 40–60 minutes
	Day 6	Kickboxing (emphasis on sparring)
	Day 7	Rest
Week 6	Day 1	Kickboxing (emphasis on competitive tactics)
	Day 2	Interval runs (with short sprints) for 40–60 minutes
	Day 3	Power training (basic exercises)
	Day 4	Kickboxing (emphasis on sparring)
	Day 5	Jogging or swimming at low intensity for 40–60 minutes
	Day 6	Kickboxing (emphasis on competitive tactics)
	Day 7	Rest
Week 7	Day 1	Kickboxing (emphasis on competitive tactics)
	Day 2	Sprint training (sprints over 60 meters, alternated with relaxed jogging)
	Day 3	Power training (basic exercises)
	Day 4	Kickboxing (emphasis on competitive tactics)
	Day 5	Interval runs for 40 minutes
	Day 6	Kickboxing (emphasis on sparring)
	Day 7	Rest
Week 8	Day 1	Kickboxing (review of competitive tactics)
	Day 2	Shadowboxing
	Day 3	Jogging at low pulse rate for 30 minutes
	Day 4	Relaxed shadowboxing
	Day 5	Rest
	Day 6	Contest
	Day 7	Rest

Other Books by Christoph Delp

English:

Fitness for Full-Contact Fighters. Berkeley, CA: Blue Snake/Frog, 2006.

Muay Thai Basics: Introductory Thai Boxing Techniques. Berkeley, CA: Blue Snake/Frog, 2006.

Muay Thai: Advanced Thai Kickboxing Techniques. Berkeley, CA: Frog, 2004.

German:

Kickboxen perfekt. Stuttgart, Germany 2007: Pietsch Verlag, 2006.

Das große Fitnessbuch. Stuttgart, Germany: Pietsch Verlag, 2006.

Kickboxen basics. Stuttgart, Germany: Pietsch Verlag, 2006.

Best Stretching. Stuttgart, Germany: Pietsch Verlag, 2005.

Fitness für Kampfsportler. Stuttgart, Germany: Pietsch Verlag, 2005.

Fitness für Männer. Stuttgart, Germany: Pietsch Verlag, 2005.

Perfektes Hanteltraining. Stuttgart, Germany: Pietsch Verlag, 2005.

Thaiboxen basics. Stuttgart, Germany: Pietsch Verlag, 2005.

Bodytraining im Fitness-Studio. Stuttgart, Germany: Pietsch Verlag, 2004.

Fit für den Strand. Stuttgart, Germany: Pietsch Verlag, 2004.

Fitness für Frauen. Stuttgart, Germany: Pietsch Verlag, 2004.

Muay Thai. Stuttgart, Germany: Pietsch Verlag, 2004.

So kämpfen die Stars. Stuttgart, Germany: Pietsch Verlag, 2003.

Bodytraining für Zuhause. Stuttgart, Germany: Pietsch Verlag, 2002.

Thai-Boxen professional. Stuttgart, Germany: Pietsch Verlag, 2002.

Bibliography

Anderson, Bob. *Stretching.* Bolinas, California: Shelter Publications, 2000.

Mack, Ferdinand. *Kickboxen—Ein Leben für den Sport.* 3. Auflage. Kernen, Germany: Sensei Verlag, 1999.

Zaar, Peter. *Kickboxen—Von den Grundlagen bis zum Hochleistungstraining.* Berlin, Germany: Sportverlag, 2000.

Online Resources

www.wakoweb.com

www.wako-deutschland.de

www.wako-austria.at

www.supermack.de

www.boxen-mit-tom.de

www.budoland.de

www.wok-fotos.de

Support from

WAKO-Deutschland e.V.

Danziger Straße 13,

91315 Höchstadt/Aisch

Germany

www.wako-deutschland.de

Book Team

Natalia Hein

Title selection: European Champion
   (2004)
German Champion
3rd Junior World Championships
Trainer: Jürgen Schorn
Club: Sportstudio Schorn (Ebern)

Vanessa Florian

Title selection: German Champion
Graduation: 1st Dan Kickboxing
1st Dan Taekwon-Do
Trainer: Peter Zaar
Club: Sportstudio Baaden (Cologne)

Andreas Weingärtner

Title selection: 3rd World Championships
   (2001)
Several-times German and International
   German Champion
Graduation: Black Belt
Trainer: Andreas Lindemann
German National coach in Semi-Contact

Giovanni Nurchi

Title selection: several-times German and
   International German Champion
5th European Championships (2004)
Graduation: Brown Belt
Trainer: Jörg Gottschalk
Club: Sportcenter Hara

Jürgen Florian

Title selection: 3rd European
    Championships (2004)
German and International German
    Champion
Graduation: Brown Belt
Trainer: Peter Zaar
Club: Sportschule Baaden

Martin Albers

Title selection: World Champion (1999)
European Champion (1998, 2000, 2002)
Graduation: 3rd Dan Kickboxing
2nd Dan Taekwon-Do, 1st Dan Jiu Jitsu
Coaches: Jochen Böckmann, Peter Zaar
Clubs: Sportstudio Böckmann
    (Cloppenburg), Sportstudion Baaden
    (Cologne)
Trainer for violence prevention,
Firm: Skills4Life (Cologne)
    www.martin-albers.de

Peter Zaar

Title selection: Several-times German
    and international German Champion,
    Team World Champion
Graduation: 6th Champion Grade WAKO
Coaches: Gustav Baaden, Georg Brückner, Ferdinand Mack
Club: Sportstudio Baaden
President WAKO e.V.
National Coach in Light-Contact
Book author: *Kickboxen—Von den Grundlagen bis
    Hochleistungstraining*

Junior Athletes Shown

Filip Ajvasov	Nico Rings
Isabelle Eberling	Peter Zaar, Jr.
Janine Steiner	Robin Neuser
Natascha Schuchardt	

Author

Christoph Delp

Diplom-Betriebswirt (master of business administration) and author

Fitness and Martial Arts trainer with fight experience in kickboxing and Muay Thai.

Some publications: *Fitness for Full-Contact Fighters (2006), Muay Thai Basics* (2006), *Advanced Muay Thai Techniques (2004), Best Stretching* (2005)

www.christophdelp.com

www.muaythai.de

Photo Acknowledgments

Photos by Firma Budoland, Peter Kruckenhauser
Oberaustraße 45, 83026 Rosenheim
(www.budoland.de): pages v, 5, 10, 123, 144, 175, 231.

Photos by JEWA-media, Jens Walbersdorf
(www.jewa-media.de): pages 68, 130.

Photos by Jürgen Schorn
(www.wok-fotos.de): *World of Kickboxing* (magazine) pages 1, 6, 25, 45, 65, 105, 121, 157, 215, 221, 222, 223, 229.

Photos by Nopphadol Viwatkamolwat
(www.astudioonline.com): page 249.

Photos by Tom Schneider
(www.boxen-mit-tom.de): page 217.

All other photos by Erwin Wenzel.

Also Available

Fitness for Full-Contact Fighters

Training for Kickboxing, Karate, Muay Thai, and Tae Kwon Do

Physical fitness is absolutely vital to success in the martial arts. It is the only way to ensure that powerful attacking techniques and rapid defensive and counterattacking techniques can be employed over the full course of a contest. Martial artists require a special fitness-training program that covers all aspects of physical performance.

In this book, author Christoph Delp presents a fitness program tailored to the martial arts. The book details the basics of fitness training and offers an in-depth description of the various elements of fitness training: flexibility, stamina, and power. The exercises are presented step by step by leading martial artists. The book focuses on planning and monitoring training and presents complete training programs for newcomers as well as those at an advanced level. There is also advice about the correct diet for martial artists. This book is an indispensable guide for martial artists of all abilities, which helps them to improve their ability to perform in training and competition.

Fitness for Full-Contact Fighters: Training for Kick-Boxing, Karate, Muay Thai, and Taekwondo

ISBN 1-58394-157-6
$22.95
Frog, Ltd./Blue Snake Books. Berkeley, California
www.northatlanticbooks.com
www.bluesnakebooks.com

Muay Thai Basics

Introductory Thai Boxing Techniques

Muay Thai, also referred to as Thai boxing, combines fitness training, self-defense, and competitive sport. In this hands-on guide, renowned trainer Christoph Delp presents the sport's history, development, rules, and equipment.

He explains basic skills, such as the correct starting position and footwork, and offers a complete list of all offensive techniques, as well as a selection of effective defensive and counterattack strategies. The techniques are presented step-by-step by Thai champions from the famous Sor. Vorapin gym in Bangkok. The training section provides detailed information about the structure, content, and planning of training regimens; this includes historical training methods, a stretching program, and training schedules. Suitable as both a self-training guide and a supplement to club training, *Muay Thai Basics* offers authoritative instruction for Thai boxers and other martial arts enthusiasts.

Muay Thai Basics: Introductory Thai Boxing Techniques

ISBN 1-58394-140-1

$19.95

Frog, Ltd./Blue Snake Books. Berkeley, California

www.northatlanticbooks.com

www.bluesnakebooks.com

Muay Thai

Advanced Thai Kickboxing Techniques

During the last twenty years, Muay Thai, also known as Thai boxing, has become popular around the world. Practitioners enjoy this martial art for fitness training, competitive sport, and self-defense.

Christoph Delp has studied intensively at many gyms and training camps in Thailand. In *Muay Thai: Advanced Thai Kickboxing Techniques,* he shares his experience of the people, history, and traditions of this exciting part of the country's extraordinary cultural heritage. Color photographs of Thai boxers demonstrate the techniques athletes must learn to succeed in professional or amateur contests, including well-proven offensive tactics as well as ways to counter an opponent's attacks. Historical Muay Thai techniques are also examined, which can be used by an experienced fighter to achieve a surprise victory.

Muay Thai: Advanced Thai Kickboxing Techniques

ISBN 1-58394-101-0

$19.95

Frog, Ltd./Blue Snake Books. Berkeley, California

www.northatlanticbooks.com

www.bluesnakebooks.com